THE EDEN WAY

Hell Gill Force

THE EDEN WAY

BY

CHARLIE EMETT

CICERONE PRESS
MILNTHORPE CUMBRIA

© C.Emett 1990
ISBN 1 85284 040 4

For
Agnes Annie Barker
'Sannie'
I called her
Grandma
and loved her dearly

Acknowledgements

This book would have been much harder to write had I not received inspiration and encouragement from so many lovely, helpful people. My gratitude to them is boundless and I hope the finished product lives up to their expectations of it.

In particular I am very much indebted to Mr & Mrs Giles Mounsey-Heysham of Castletown, whose enigmatic ancestor set the ball rolling, for their hospitality to Shalom Hermon and the members of the "Quest For The Jew Stone" tour as well as to myself. Sincere thanks.

To David Hay of Cumberland News thanks for your help and good luck with your own book. Thanks, also to Mr I.Plenderleith, Chief Administrative Officer, Carlisle Civic Centre for guiding me through Carlisle past and present and to Alan Edmundson for making that part of the journey such fun.

Carlisle and Darlington libraries, Durham County Library and the North Yorkshire County Library, York were all very helpful - so thanks.

Heaven be praised for people like the Rector of Wetheral and Mr & Mrs L.H.Ferguson, whose friendship is greatly valued, as is that of the "hard news girl with the soft heart," Fiona Armstrong. I am very appreciative of the unstinting interest, advice and encouragement given by Mr E.P.Ecroyd and to Mrs Stapleton for allowing me to explore the private left bank of Eden Gorge. Also to Mr Joe Taylor, gamekeeper, ghillie and most happy fellow and to John and Alice Brown who know how to fill a man's stomach.

Many thanks also go to Romany Bain, Jean Anderson, accomplished actress; Hazel Chew, matron at the Sue Ryder Home, Acorn Bank; T.S. and Mrs Pollock of Winderwath, Norman Dunn of Whinfell, one of the best gamekeepers in the business, and Joanne Burgess of the Cumberland and Westmorland Herald, Penrith.

The replacement Jew Stone would have remained a broken dream, like the original but for the positive involvement of Guy and Giles

Thompson of Hanging Lund, so special thanks for special people.

Thank you Bet for letting me out and your tolerance during the writing.

Straight line walks, unlike circulars depend on back-up, vehicular support and Ken Hudson supplied this and with Gordon Dally provided photographs. Thank you both.

Thank you Bill Bamlett and Ruth for being such good companions.

Extra special thanks must to go Ron Dodsworth, who not only drew the maps but for many years now has been a great hiking companion. We journeyed along every bit of the Eden Valley Way together; and as we walked we talked and our conversations were richer than tea or wine.

My grateful thanks to Barbara Barker who had the unenviable task of converting my handwriting into type and did it so well.

If I have omitted anyone it is unintentional and I apologise.

Charlie Emett, 1990

A copy of a painting in Castletown, showing that the river was once used by boats. (Courtesy of Mounsey-Heysham)

Contents

Introduction 9

1: Rockcliffe Marsh to Carlisle 14

2: Carlisle 25

3: Carlisle to Wetheral 50

4: Wetheral to Armathwaite 62

5: Armathwaite to Kirkoswald 77

6: Kirkoswald to Langwathby 89

7: Langwathby to Appleby 102

8: Appleby to Warcop 117

9: Warcop to Kirkby Stephen 133

10: Kirkby Stephen to Black Fell Moss via
    The Roman Road 141

11: Kirkby Stephen to Black Fell Moss via Wild Boar Fell 160

12: Black Fell Moss to Kirkby Stephen via
    Mallerstang Edge and the Nine Standards 169

Envoi 178

Selected Bibliography 179

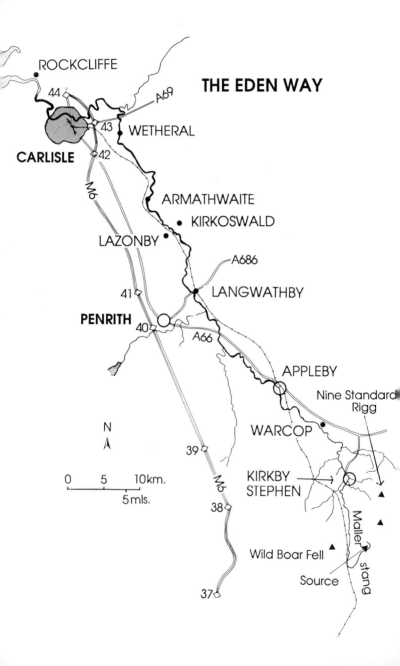

Introduction

It all began on the Ides of March, 1850, when William Mounsey of the wealthy Mounsey-Heysham family decided to trace the Eden from its entry into the Solway to its lonely birthplace below Hugh Seat high on Black Fell Moss.

His home was at Rockcliffe, north-west of Carlisle, where his parents were wealthy landowners living on the Castletown Estate, the family seat. He was a man of high intelligence, well-versed in the classics, who could converse fluently in Greek, Latin, Persian and Welsh as well as his mother tongue.

On May 28th 1825, he purchased his commission as an Ensign in the 30th (Cambridgeshire) Regiment and on January 4th, 1833, purchased his promotion to Lieutenant in a vacancy in the 15th (Yorkshire East Riding) Regiment. On April 14th, 1837, he purchased his Captaincy in a vacancy in the 4th (King's Own) Regiment. The 4th (King's Own) Regiment became The King's Own Royal Regiment (Lancaster) in 1881 and is now part of The King's Own Royal Border Regiment.

At the time of William Mounsey's Army service each officer's progress was noted in a log. Should an officer excel or behave reprehensibly his conduct was duly recorded. Should he fail to impress, nothing was recorded in his log. There were no entries shown in the log against Mounsey's name. With an undistinguished Army career behind him he sold his commission in 1844.

He spent much of his time travelling in Egypt and the Middle East where his interest in Persia developed as his fascination with astrology and the occult deepened. Mysteries fascinated him to such an extent that he often wrapped simple statements in enigmatic language, frequently signing his work with the word "Mounsey" presented backwards. Mounsey regularly used hermetic and alchemical signals and this was very likely his mischievous way of cocking a snoot at a general public that did not understand him. He was a Gentile but since he wore his beard long in the manner of a Jew he became known as 'the Carlisle Jew'.

If his Army career was undistinguished, William Mounsey's civilian life was, to say the least, extraordinary. He became a solicitor and had means sufficient enough for him to gratify his eccentricities. His decision, early in 1850, to seek the source of the River Eden caused many people to think that he had taken leave of his senses. As the mallard flies there are sixty miles between the Eden's source and its mouth but for anyone following its writhing course - which becomes particularly serpentine in its lower reaches - the distance to be covered is nearer seventy-five miles. To embark on such a venture in the mid-19th century strong determination was of the essence, for the journey was a lonely, arduous and hazardous one. William Mounsey had both the guts and the will: if anyone could accomplish this pilgrimage, he could.

The walk was a success; and to commemorate his remarkable achievement he had a monument erected on the brow of Red Gill overlooking an ancient sheep fold near the source of the infant stream which would soon become the Eden.

The monument, of Dent marble, measured 7 feet by 7.75 inches by 3 inches and contained texts in Latin and Greek. The Latin inscription, translated, read:- "William Mounsey, a lone traveller, having commenced his journey at the mouth and finished it at the source, fulfilled his vow to the genius and nymphs of the Eden on the 15th March, 1850".

The opposite side of the column carried two Greek quotations:- "Seek the river of the soul - whence it springs, when thou hast served the body in a certain order - when thou has acknowledged thy duty to the sacred Scriptures - thou shalt be raised again to the order from which thou art fallen" and "Let us flee with ships to our dear native land: for we have a country from which we have come and our father is there".

Two symbols were carved into the marble. One looks like three capital Ts with the foot of each touching. The other is the Star of David. The T represents the tau occult sigil or sign, which is the earliest form of cross. It is a combination of a Greek letter and an Arabic number and represents the link between earthly and eternal life. Three Ts touching become the Holy Trinity. The Star of David, sometimes called the Seal of Solomon, is a common early sigil and is the graphic origin of the four most common signs of the four elements, air, earth, fire and water, with an esoteric fifth element, usually termed the quintessence, the blank space in the middle representing the invisible spirit world.

William Mounsey's inclusion of the fifth element and with the symbol of the three capital Ts touching at the foot on the monument emphasises his interest in the invisible spirit world.

Because the Star of David was prominently displayed on the monument and since the person who had it put there looked like a Jew, the monument came to be known as the Jew Stone.

The Jew Stone remained undisturbed overlooking Red Gill until 1870 when some navvies employed on the construction of the Settle-Carlisle line came across it while they were out for a walk one Sunday. Being unable to read the texts they vandalised it.

For more than three quarters of a century the Jew Stone, now in three pieces, remained in situ, forgotten by all but a few. It was not until after World War II that any serious attempt was made to restore it to its former state. Then one day Kirkby Stephen Fell Rescue Team acquired a new stretcher and the members were keen to test it in a simulated exercise. Someone pointed out that the pieces of the Jew Stone together weighed roughly the same as an average-sized man, so why not rescue it and bring it to Kirkby Stephen with a view to having it repaired and returned to the fell? The rescue was a success but the Jew Stone was found to be beyond repair.

In an attempt to raise sufficient funds for a replacement Jew Stone the author, with his friend and fellow walker Stuart Dean for company and with another close friend, Ken Hudson, acting as support, spent the entire Easter weekend of 1986 treading in the steps of William Mounsey.

The walk was superb and we had a ball. The Eden, Cumbria's longest and to many eyes, its most beautiful river, was at its beguiling best with every bend bringing fresh delights. Our exhilarating journey through the rich farmland of Edenvale took us past many comfortable villages and townships, most of which had strong historical associations. Local wildlife was much in evidence; and the valley is an ornithologist's paradise. With little to jar the senses the overwhelming impression was of neatness and harmony.

On the evening of the last day of the walk Stuart and I stood on a huge snowdrift which completely covered the narrow gully down which the beck called Red Gill poured. From the drift's lower end snow broth issued. It poured noisily from a cavern it had worn for itself on the drift's underside and tumbled down a rough bed soon to be joined by other feeders and become the Eden.

The spring which was the Eden's principal source lay somewhere under the drift, close to its top end. We were standing as close to that spring as we could, with safety.

Earlier that afternoon the weather had broken and we had encountered snow showers. Now daylight was beginning to drain from a threatening grey sky and the temperature was falling fast. We would have to get cracking if we were to be off the fell before darkness.

Our feet were wet, we were tired and beginning to feel the cold; but we had accomplished what we had set out to do and it was a great feeling.

Rockcliffe Church

1: Rockcliffe Marsh to Carlisle

Length of section:	6 miles
Total distance:	6 miles
Map:	O.S. Landranger 85
Handy hostelries:	Redfern Inn, Kingmoor Road, St. Anne's Hill, Carlisle.

Route Directions

The walk begins on the north bank of the river at Rockcliffe Marsh, which is easily reached from Demesne Farm by going down a short lane to the right of the farmhouse then right again along a farm track to where it bends half-right. Here take the short path to the left onto the end of an embankment. Continue along the top of the embankment, which runs parallel to the river and close to it. Where the embankment curves to the right, away from the river, following the landward edge of Rockcliffe Marsh, leave it and continue straight ahead onto the marsh until you are opposite Burghmarsh Point on the river's southern bank. This is easily identified from the north of the river because, as seen from there, Burghmarsh Point marks the end of the shoreline. Here Eden and Solway merge and it is from here, for the purist, that this splendid walk begins.

Between Demesne Farm and the start of the walk you pass through several gates. It is very important that you close them behind you because otherwise there is a chance that cattle will wander towards the river or the marsh where they could get into difficulties.

Retrace your steps to the end of the embankment and leave it through a gate. Go down the tree-lined track to Demesne Farm where go through a gate on your right and past the front of the house on raised ground with a wooden slope on your right. Where a sign says public footpath to Rockcliffe Cross go through a gate on the right and up a bank, then down to the edge of the river.

With the river on your right just keep walking upstream towards the cliffs on which Rockcliffe stands. Soon a gate is seen ahead. Go

Rockcliffe to Carlisle

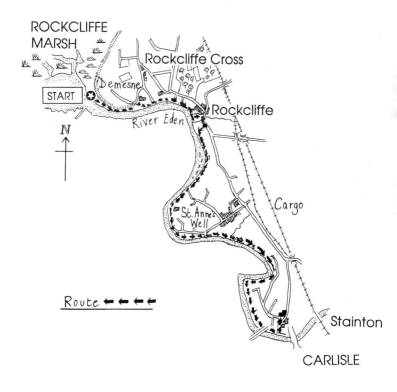

ROCKCLIFFE
MARSH

Rockcliffe Cross

Demesne

START

Rockcliffe

River Eden

N

Cargo

St. Anne's
Well

Route ← ← ← ←

Stainton

CARLISLE

through it and climb up a lane which leads to the top of the cliffs. The way now becomes a tarmac road which passes some cottages before going downhill towards a feeder stream. Cross the feeder on a footbridge and follow it downstream for a short distance to where it joins the river.

The way is now along the river bank on the riverside of a wire fence for almost as far as some islands where, slightly set back from the river just to the right of a bank on which there is a little, old, red-roofed hut, a wooden footbridge over a feeder stream is crossed. Return to the river and continue along its edge, making a small detour at one point to cross another small feeder. The way is past the front of a solitary renovated dwelling, Fish House, and, on approaching the inside of a long loop in the river, past St. Anne's Well on your left.

A mile upstream of St. Anne's Well the downstream end of a wood is reached. The way goes through it, along a narrow path that keeps close to the water, undulating slightly as it goes along. When the river is in spate this part of the route becomes flooded, in which case continue by the top edge of the wood and return to the route at the wood's upper end.

Soon after passing some hen huts another feeder stream is crossed on a footbridge and the route then bifurcates, the lower branch going through a long, narrow wood at about water level, the other climbing uphill and along the top edge of the wood, crossing obstructing field boundaries by means of stiles. At the wood's upper end both paths meet at the bottom of a steep slope and remain as one for the rest of the section.

Cross the bottom of a field, exit through a gate and keep going to where the river makes a sharp bend, where cross a stile on your right.

Keep to the riverside for almost two miles to where a disused railway bridge crosses the river. Go under it, through a gate in a fence underneath it and immediately climb onto an embankment. Walk along it to where, at its upper end, what looks like the bed of a beck comes downhill on your left. This is really a short, steep lane which will bring you to a tarmac road. Turn right along this road and go along it to a junction with Kingmoor Road. There, on your left, is to be found the Redfern Inn, the pub closest to this end of the section.

The Background Story

Had Britain been a tropical island this walk would have started in a mangrove swamp. But since it lies in a temperate zone, the Eden Valley Way begins on a salt marsh which is the temperate equivalent. Rockcliffe Marsh is where the now tidal Eden pours into the Solway Firth cutting its way through a vast expanse of mud and sand to merge with the waters of the River Esk before being swallowed by the Irish Sea.

Rockcliffe Marsh, which has been declared an Area of Outstanding Natural Beauty along with some forty square miles of the Solway Firth, is an important winter haunt for wildfowl. Wildfowling has been pursued there for centuries, firstly for food but latterly for sport. It is a traditional sport all along the Solway and the wildfowlers find the attraction of the pursuit compelling despite frequently freezing conditions. Shooting permits are limited to prevent too much disturbance to the wild geese on the "merse" and, thanks to this restriction relations between the wildfowlers and the conservationists are very good.

At high water of an ordinary spring tide only about one tenth of the marsh is left exposed. Wild geese graze on the higher ground where the grass is more abundant. Deep drainage channels and pools mark this "merse' where lapwing, oystercatcher, snipe, redshank, mallard and shelduck breed and foxes, stoats and hares rove. It has been like this for centuries and is likely to remain so because in any civilized country the two kinds of habitat least changed by man are those of the mountain and the coast.

Sheep were once wintered on Rockcliffe Marsh but following three terrible disasters within a quarter of a century this is no longer the case. In 1926, at the height of a gale, a high tide flooded the marsh and 900 sheep were drowned. A similar number suffered the same fate when, in 1937, the marsh was again flooded. Then, in 1949, many more sheep lost their lives when once more the whole of the marsh found itself inundated by a high tide. The local farmers decided enough was enough. They determined that never again would sheep winter graze Rockcliffe Marsh; and, to date, they never have.

After Morecambe Bay, the Solway Firth, of which Rockcliffe Marsh is part, is the second most important estuary for waders in Britain. Usually the pink-footed geese are the first to arrive. They appear in September but their stay is a short one. The grey lags arrive about mid-October and are the predominant wintering species.

The barnacle geese wintering in the area represent the entire breeding population of Spitzbergen. Several thousand of them may be seen grazing at the same time. Beautiful birds with white faces and black heads, barnacle geese owe their name to a medieval myth. Our ancestors, unaware of the Spitzbergen breeding grounds, thought that, unlike other birds that came from eggs, barnacle geese developed from goose barnacles that were washed ashore attached to driftwood. So persistent was the myth that less than seventy years ago barnacle geese were eaten during Lent in certain parts of Ireland in the belief that they were more fish than fowl. The geese feed almost entirely on grass.

Three species of black geese can be found in Britain and all frequent the Solway Firth. The Canada goose is the largest, is browner than the barnacle and has less white on its face. The barnacle, which is a protected species, is smaller than the Canada goose but larger than the Brent, which has an all black head and no wing bars. All our other geese are greys.

From Rockcliffe Marsh there is a traditional river crossing to the Eden's southern bank, a ford that has all the requirements to be accepted as the site of the battle of Gwen Ystrat, or White Strath, where that great warrior Urien defeated a numerically superior party of Picts intent on pillaging the Solway coast of Rheged.

During the twenty years following the death of King Arthur after the battle of Camlann in 537AD the Angles, Saxons and Jutes almost completed the conquest of Britain: almost but not quite. There remained one core of fierce resistance and the Kingdom of Rheged was at its heart.

It covered all of what was modern Cumberland, North Westmorland and that part of Northumberland not conquered by the Angles. Carlisle was in Rheged but was not its capital. That distinction went to a much more secure place, Llwyfenyd, the hidden valley of the Lyvennet, a tributary of the Eden which flows into it near Temple Sowerby. It was here that Urien and his son, Owain, had their headquarters; possibly at Crosby Ravensworth, a place with Arthurian associations.

Urien had established himself as ruler of Rheged in the power struggle following Arthur's death. He had many of Arthur's qualities and was a great leader. His praises have been sung in eight poems by Taliesin who was a genuine historical figure highly respected for his professionalism. Taliesin was Urien's personal bard, his job being to produce poetry in praise of his master. It is from one of these poems that we know about the battle of Gwen Ystrat where Urien gained a famous victory, catching the Picts off-guard as they crossed the river.

Time and time again during the Border troubles this traditional ford was the setting for numerous skirmishes with cattle rustlers and when whisky smuggling was rife many a smuggler clashed with the excise men at that very spot.

The largest number of men to cross the ford in one day did so in the autumn of 1745 with Bonnie Prince Charlie at their head. He had landed in Argyllshire on July 25th of that year with seven followers to lead a rising to restore his father to the British throne and, with men rallying to him daily, had occupied Edinburgh on September 17th. On November 8th, at the head of the main Scottish army, he crossed the Esk into England and on November 9th, using the ford from Rockcliffe Marsh, crossed the Eden on his way to Moorhouse village where his forces spent the night. On November 10th he began the siege of Carlisle and his ill-fated excursion into England.

In 150AD Ptolemy, the astronomer, called our river "Itona"; to the Old British it was "Ituna" and to the Cumbri of Rheged it was "Idon". But the name by which it has been known for longest and which suits it best is Eden, a Hebrew word meaning "delight".

The Eden is a spate river subject to fluctuating levels, especially early in the year when the salmon season begins. The best of the salmon fishing is in January, February and March and again during

Salmon fishers

September and October. The season begins on January 15th and ends on October 14th. In the lower reaches the fishing is primarily for brown trout, salmon and sea trout but there are also plenty of coarse fish to be caught, especially in winter when fishing for chub and dace is very popular. The season for trout is from March 15th to September 30th and for coarse fish from June 16th to March 15th. From its mouth for seven miles upstream the fishing is controlled by the Carlisle Angling Association.

Situated on the Eden's north bank the remote village of Rockcliffe is the first or last village along the Eden Valley Way, depending upon your direction of walk. It sits high above flood level on the red cliff from which it gets its name.

Rockcliffe church, St. Mary's, has a tall, graceful spire that has had its share of ups and downs. The original one was demolished and rebuilt to a height of one hundred feet in 1881. Then, on November 8th, 1899, it was hit by lightning during a violent thunderstorm and had to be built once again. A plaque in the north isle is in memory of Post Captain William Mounsey, 1765-1830, of the Royal Navy who, in thirty-five years of service, captured thirty-one enemy ships. One was the frigate Lafurieuse and for this action he received the thanks of the Admiralty and a special gold medal from George III. Close to the path through the churchyard there is a solid wheel-head cross which dates from the 10th or 11th century.

The village has a school, which was built in 1871 and enlarged in 1890, a post office-cum-general store and a pub with a name that should please people on both sides of the border, The Crown and Thistle.

From Rockcliffe the way follows the river bank that appears to be slightly higher than the pasture behind it which, according to some local people, is frequently flooded when the river in spate meets a flowing tide. I found that following several rainy days, the pasture was soggy and pock-marked with broad pools. The river's edge was the driest bit. As for the Eden herself, brown flood water had swollen her to a frightening size. On previous walks along this part of the river the water level had been a lot lower and the rate of flow a little less speedy. This time I found, as I progressed upstream, that drainage channels which were usually narrow enough to leap had become vast sheets of water far too wide to jump and detours were the order of the day.

Unlike so many other English waterways whose upper reaches hold out a promise which their lower reaches cannot sustain, fair Eden meets its destiny with the Solway unblemished. Man's hand has not despoiled its final miles. It has been allowed, in its maturity, to flow through a pastoral and wooded landscape that is delightful. Right from the start on Rockcliffe Marsh you will be impressed by the walk's excellence.

A short half-mile upstream from some islands on a broad bend, in a field close to the river's northern bank, stands a solitary recently re-roofed building known as the Fish House. Once Carlisle Corporation, by virtue of an ancient grant, held certain fishing rights along a stretch of the Eden, between a place near Cargo to Etterby. This right is no longer exercised but until almost a century ago a complimentary fish dinner was held in Fish House for the Mayor and Corporation.

There are plaques on the rear walls commemorating the visits of four different mayors, one is dated 1751 and another records the visit of "the first freely elected Mayor of Carlisle" in June 1837.

It was near Fish House that I once came upon some magnificent whooper swans. I was up wind of them and they knew I was there. Yet not until I had got quite close did they show signs of taking flight. The airlift began rather slowly to the accompaniment of loud trumpeting. A few on the outer edge of the flock became airborne. More followed and still more, rising quickly now, each hurrying as though not wishing to be last off the ground. What a splendid sight it was! At least thirty pairs of whoopers in circular flight some twenty feet above the stubble. For several seconds they circled in seemingly effortless flight. Then, as if on cue, they made a mass landing in the next field.

Once whooper swans were British breeding birds but now they are winter visitors from Northern Europe and Russia. Unlike the mute swan, which has a gently curved neck, the whooper's, like the Bewick's, neck is carried stiffly erect when on the ground and thrust forward when in flight. The birds are large ones, frequently measuring five feet from tip of tail to neb end.

Swans frequently feed on the low-lying northern side of the river hereabouts. The other side of the water is not so inviting for them. Being a steep, wooded slope, it holds no interest for hungry swans.

Following the inside of a very long bend in the river's course a muddy track that soon becomes a lane confined by hedges eventually turns away from the river to the village of Cargo, less than half a mile distant. This small collection of farms, houses and bungalows gets its name from Carig Howe, meaning "the rocky eminence".

On November 10th, 1745, a contingent of Bonnie Prince Charlie's troops passed through Cargo, crossed the river and went to Grinsdale to support the main army which had crossed at Rockcliffe the previous day. Search as I might, I could not make out where the crossing had taken place. The wonder is that it took place at all for the whole of this stretch of water is wide, deep and very fast-flowing.

Of the three villages on the Eden's southern bank between Carlisle and the Solway, Grinsdale lies closest to the city. All three - Grinsdale, Kirkandrews-on-Eden and Beaumont - can be reached quite easily on foot simply by walking along the river bank. Grinsdale is a small farming community of a few houses, some farms and a small pebble-dashed church which stands among trees on raised ground above the river and some distance from the village. The Royal Arms of George III are displayed on its west wall. Its setting is very pleasant but views from it in some directions are somewhat spoiled by electricity pylons.

From a hilltop across the river from Grinsdale and a little down-stream of it you get the first glimpse of Carlisle two miles distant. You see it through a gap in the trees that grow in profusion along the steep river bank below. The winding river occupies most of the foreground with flattish, open country beyond and beyond that, Carlisle.

From the hilltop vantage point you can see among the electricity pylons near Cargo a great many overhead power columns of a different design. The columns and the power cables they carried had once played an essential part in Europe's largest marshalling yard, Kingmoor. Today hardly any marshalling is done there and the promised prosperity the yard had been designed to bring to the area has faded away.

It all began in 1961 when Beeching built it for the trans-shipment of rail-borne traffic to B.R.S. parcel vans. Sadly, no sooner had the yard become operational than container vans began to be used instead. Almost overnight the reality became a memory and Kingmoor was finished.

In building Kingmoor millions of tons of earth were carted away, many roads and bridges were removed and huge cuttings con-structed. As an integral part of this work the line between Etterby and Longtown was straightened, allowing expresses to thunder along this section of track at 120mph in one direction and almost as fast in the other.

A large maintenance depot is just about all that is left of this white elephant; and this is due to close by the time this book appears. A lot of the work-force at the maintenance depot began their working lives at Upperby. From there they went to the Canal Road depot on the south side of the Eden. Then they came to Kingmoor. Now that this depot is about to close, employment has been found for many of them at Upperby, thus completing the circle.

A further two miles or so, as the river bends, the path leads very pleasantly to Etterby and the end of the first section. The terrain is flat, the going easy and where wire fences cross the way, stiles are provided. The walk follows the river's edge, between it and a grassed-over embankment which parallels the river's course. Without the embankment, in times of flooding, large tracts of pasture to the sheltered side of it would be under water.

Within a few hundred yards of the end of the first section is an embankment which leads directly onto a bridge which once carried a railway across the river. This bridge is the furthest downstream of all the Eden's bridges.

Immediately upstream of it, on the south bank, stands a disused and decaying power-station. Until 1982, when it was demolished, its tall chimney was a local landmark. Because of the chimney's position it could not be blasted down in Fred Dibner manner. It had to be brought down the hard way, brick by brick.

While the power-station was operational fish living in that part of the river warmed by the generators' waste warm water grew much larger than those from other parts of the river. But surprisingly those whoppers were not eagerly sought after: the warm water also made them very soft in texture and therefore less acceptable.

The site of the power-station, once it has been cleared, is to be turned into an industrial park.

At the end of a tall embankment which runs alongside the river immediately upstream of the bridge you turn into what looks like the bed of a shallow stream but which is really a path, climb it to a tarmac road.

2:   Carlisle

Length of section:	2 miles
Total distance:	8 miles
Map:	O.S. Landranger 85
Handy hostelries:	Carlisle has an abundance of cafés and pubs

Route Directions

From the lane leading uphill from the river which was used at the end of section one, turn right along Etterby Road for almost half a mile, crossing, en route, a bridge over the main railway line to Scotland. Soon after crossing the bridge the river can be seen below, because Etterby Road keeps close to the top of Etterby Scaur at the foot of which the river flows. (N.B. The footpath below the Scaur is in poor repair and when the river is high, is under water.) Where an easily identified tarmac lane leads down to the river take it and continue along it, by the riverside to Eden Bridge. Go under the bridge and, still keeping close to the river bank, continue through Rickerby Park to its eastern boundary, the end of the section.

The Background Story

The city of Carlisle, before Agricola established a base there around 78-80AD, was nothing more than a native settlement. A few years earlier Petillius Cerialis brought an army over Stainmore and is thought to have reached this settlement. But it is to Agricola that the credit must go for the beginning of its development.

The settlement was sited where the castle now is and the fort that housed Agricola's garrison, a turf and wood construction, was built where the cathedral stands today. Called Luguvalium, it was controlled by the Romans for more than 350 years.

About 100AD the fort was rebuilt, enlarged and strengthened. Then, some thirty years later, when the Emperor Hadrian was forced to abandon the Scottish conquests and decided to consolidate the

Carlisle

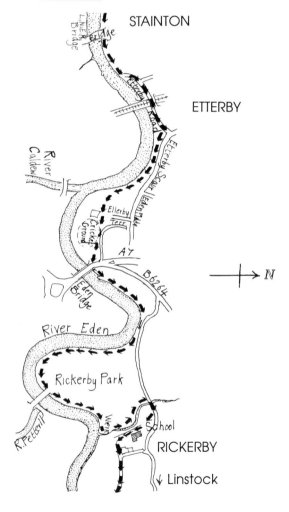

STAINTON

ETTERBY

→ N

↓ Linstock

RICKERBY

frontier of his empire across the narrow Solway-Tyne isthmus with a defence system which came to be known as Hadrian's Wall, its garrison was transferred to a newly built stone fort at Petriana (Stanwix) on the north bank of the Eden. This fort, the largest camp along the Wall, housed a regiment of cavalry 1,000 strong which was always kept in a state of readiness for instant action anywhere along the western section of this important line of defence. It was the Roman equivalent of the U.S. 7th Cavalry during the Indian wars. Luguvalium itself was demolished and replanned as a civil settlement.

For 250 years Luguvalium was the principal administrative centre of the western section of the northern Roman frontier and during that period its inhabitants enjoyed a standard of comfort, hygiene, wealth and security not to be equalled again until the present century. Some of the streets were paved, many of the houses were well-built, some were timbered and had tiled roofs and there was a drainage system.

In accordance with Roman custom the dead could not be buried in inhabited areas. They were interred in cemeteries outside the seventy acres comprising Luguvalium, in places like today's Botcherby, east of the city.

From the forum roads radiated south along today's English Street and Botchergate, to the north along Scotch Street and over the Eden and to the west towards Caldergate.

Roman influence on Luguvalium was so pronounced that it determined the future shape of Carlisle and its road pattern to the present day. Carlisle Cross or the Market Cross stands on the site of the Roman forum or market place. Ever since Roman times this site has been used whenever important notices have been read, proclamations declaimed, and lists of citizens who have died in epidemics have had to be posted. Until recently mileage to and from Carlisle has been measured from there.

For the three hundred or so years immediately following the Roman evacuation of England, between 383AD and 400AD, Carlisle continued to reap great benefit from their occupation. So much so that when in 685AD Saint Cuthbert visited Carlisle he was proudly shown round the walls of the city and had pointed out to him a fountain of remarkable workmanship the Romans had built.

By the time of Saint Cuthbert's visit the name Luguvalium had been corrupted in common use to Luel. Later the Celtic word Caer, meaning fort, was added and in the vernacular of the inhabitants the place became known as Caer-luel, though scholars used the word "Lugubalia" until about 1400.

Towards the end of the ninth century, at a time when many of the northern tribes were enmeshed in bitter power struggles, the heathen Danes sailed up the Solway. They came, stayed for a comparatively short time, and were an unmitigated disaster for Carlisle. For, in 875AD, under Halfdan they sacked it with such brutality that for the next two hundred years no one could differentiate between town and surrounding country. The walls were demolished, the town burned and every man, woman and child was killed. As for the Danish pillagers, they moved on, northwards and eastwards into Northumbria and Yorkshire.

The Norse arrived in 925AD. Like the Danes they came up the Solway but unlike them their invasion was a far more penetrating and less warlike one. They came not directly from Norway but by way of Ireland from where they had learned a little about Christianity. Gradually they settled along the Eden and in the Cumbrian dales living in scattered farmsteads and small hamlets. They drained marshlands to provide sheltered pastures and crop-bearing fields. They enclosed these fields with stone walls which, in time, produced the valley bottom landscapes of today.

At that time Carlisle and its surrounding district was linked with Galloway and Strathclyde and known as the Kingdom of Cumbria. Following the defeat of Dunmail, King of Cumbria, by the Saxon King Edmund, the Kingdom of Cumbria was given to Malcolm I, King of the Scots and remained under Scottish rule until about 1070. For this reason Carlisle does not appear in William the Conqueror's Domesday Book.

In 1072 Gospatric, Earl of Northumberland, when deprived of his earldom, handed over Carlisle to his son, Dolfin. Gospatric had taken possession of it two years earlier and Dolfin became its ruler for a further 20 years until 1092 when William Rufus drove him out. It was William Rufus who restored the town, built the castle and brought Carlisle firmly back onto English soil where it has remained ever since, the last city to become English.

It was William Rufus's determination to have a secure frontier between England and Scotland that had prompted him to restore Carlisle town and build the castle; and when this had been accomplished he repopulated the area with country folk from the south, people whose loyalties he could trust. Castle and city were kept separate.

When William Rufus died he was succeeded by Henry I, whose wife, Edith, was the daughter of King Malcolm of Scotland; and she, being a Scot, had an interest in England's boundary with her father's kingdom. Henry I was never other than friendly towards the Scots yet when he visited Carlisle in 1122 he decided to strengthen the castle, then a palisaded, wooden structure, and fortify the city. He founded the diocese of Carlisle in 1133 and the Augustinian priory, which he had established in 1102, became a cathedral dedicated to the Blessed Virgin Mary.

Henry I died in 1135 and the Scots under King David seized Carlisle once more and strengthened its defences. For twenty years they held it, King David dying in the castle in 1153. His grandson, Malcolm, succeeded him.

Five years later, in 1158, Henry II, who had already seized back Cumberland, Westmorland and Northumberland from Scotland, visited Carlisle hoping to gain the allegiance of its citizens and granted the city's first charter.

When Malcolm died and his brother followed him as King of Scotland in 1165 he disputed Henry's claim to Carlisle and in 1174 besieged the city but without success.

Throughout the reign of Richard I and almost all that of John who succeeded him, the Scots continued to press their claim for Carlisle and eventually, in 1216, won it, thanks to the unjust and heavy taxation brought about by King John's misrule. That year King

Alexander II of Scotland decided that the time had come to cross the border and take the city and the castle. He did so without much trouble.

King John died soon afterwards and the following year Henry III ordered Alexander to stop creating border strife and go back to Scotland. Substantial financial compensation accompanied this order and this pleased Alexander who, in the vernacular, "took it and buggered off."

For the follow eighty years Carlisle was peaceful. In 1233 Franciscan, (grey) and Dominican, (black) friars settled there, the convent of the former being outside the city wall.

In 1251 Henry III gave Carlisle a second charter to replace the one granted to it in 1158 which somehow had been destroyed by fire. This, too, was lost in the great fire of May 1292, in which most of Carlisle was gutted. In 1293 a third charter was granted to the city by Edward I who had stayed there in 1280 and was aware of its potential as a border fortress. These charters were very important to Carlisle because they authorised the citizens to have their own municipal government, hold local courts and to control trading and markets.

Not without good cause was Edward I nicknamed "hammer of the Scots". His detestation of them was only exceeded by his determination to impose English sovereignty on their homeland. His intransigence towards them inflamed more hatred in the Borderlands than any other single individual had done either before or since. He turned Carlisle into a major military centre, repaired the castle and turned it into a palace as well as a stronghold.

In March, 1296, the Earl of Buchan, at the head of an army of 40,000 men, crossed into England and attacked Carlisle, whose citizens and garrison resisted strongly. During the confusion a Scot, who had been imprisoned on suspicion of spying, escaped and set fire to the prison. Fanned by a strong wind the flames spread quickly. While the men fought the fire the women hurtled stones from the battlements and poured boiling water on the Scots. The day was saved when, during an attempt to set alight one of the gates, the leader of the fire-raisers was impaled on a hook and while thus suspended had spears driven into his writhing body. This disheartened the Scots who, the next day, abandoned their attack and returned home.

The early loyalty of Scottish hero Robert the Bruce fluctuated between Edward I and the Scottish patriots under Wallace. With the passing years he tended to side increasingly with the latter and in 1306, after murdering his rival "Red" Comyn, he emerged as a national leader. That same year he was crowned King Robert I of Scotland at Scone.

Edward, now old, sick and embittered because his dream of becoming Master of the whole of Britain was still unfulfilled, was incensed. He came north with an army intent on entering Scotland and taking the Scottish crown by force.

At Carlisle he stood among the ruins of the cathedral, still charred from the great fire of 1292, to hear the Papal legate excommunicate Bruce "with bell, book and candle". Then he moved on.

Further progress was painfully slow. The planned route was north-east to Burgh-by-Sands then north to cross the Eden at the Rockcliffe Marsh ford. But a few days after leaving Carlisle he had covered only six miles reaching the edge of empty, windswept Burch Marsh, a mile north of Burgh-by-Sands. In that lonely place he died and his invasion of Scotland was brought to an abrupt end.

At the battle of Bannockburn in 1314, the result of which confirmed the establishment of the Scottish Kingdom over which control had been disputed since 1296, only one English commander acquitted himself well enough to gain the praise of the Scottish victor, Robert Bruce. That man was Sir Andrew de Harcla.

Spurred on by his famous victory, Bruce attacked Carlisle the following year, determined to capture it because his father had commanded it from 1295 to 1297.

The siege of Carlisle was one of the most famous sieges in the history of the Border wars. Carlisle was well fortified. Its gates, strong in themselves, were supplemented by heavy stockades. As, led by Bruce himself, the hosts of Scottish clansmen advanced on the city Sir Andrew stood on the castle's battlements and prepared to repel the onslaught. With him were "Kendal archers, all in green."

Bruce, now at the height of his fame and menacingly confident, attacked, "scattering fire and slaughter in his path." The Kendal archers countered and shot darts and arrows thick as rain on the assailants. Beaten off, Bruce set siege to the city and brought into action balistas and battering rams. Built on the cross-bow principle, those balistas were capable of hurling stone balls, eight inches in diameter and weighing about 15lbs. But not all worked as intended. At least one of the balistas was faulty and threw its missiles backwards onto Bruce's own men.

Despite the huge catapults, battering rams, spears, axes and the size of his army Bruce made no headway against Sir Andrew's spirited defence. For eleven days the siege continued, then Bruce called off his army and retired, leaving all his equipment behind.

In recognition of Sir Andrew's signal service in saving Carlisle, Edward II issued a proclamation which commanded "all the inhabitants of the Counties of Cumberland, Westmorland and Lancaster to give him their attendance and obedience." This was equivalent to nominating him Lord Warden of The Western Marches. The word "March" means a border frontier and from it the title Marquis has evolved.

In 1322 some English barons, headed by the Earl of Lancaster, rebelled against the Crown. Others, including Roger de Clifford, joined them and their combined forces gathered at Borough Bridge to face the King's troops led by Sir Andrew de Harcla.

Lancaster tried to bribe Sir Andrew but without success.

Battle commenced and Sir Andrew's superior military skill soon had the rebellious barons fleeing in disarray. The revolt was crushed and Sir Andrew was created Earl of Carlisle. The appointment placed Sir Andrew in a precarious position because it caused jealousy among his rivals.

Taking full advantage of Edward II's weakness as a monarch, Bruce, having established himself as King of Scotland, set about ravaging the northern counties of England in merciless revenge for all that Scotland had suffered at the hands of the English.

Sir Andrew, realising the futility of this continuous warfare and

The River Eden near Armathwaite
Photo: Walt Unsworth

seeing for himself the suffering of the local people who had "nothing but their naked bodies to give to the King's service,' attempted to come to an understanding with the Scots. His motives were loyal but at Westminster evil rumours were allowed to spread around the court and, as intended, reached the ears of the King.

At first Edward II resolved to command Sir Andrew to present himself at court so that he, the King, could hear what the man had to say before making judgement. This, at least, would have shown some fairness. But the vacillating monarch had second thoughts and ordered a special commission to seize Sir Andrew and charge him with high treason.

Sir Andrew, at his post in Carlisle castle, got no warning. His arrest was sudden and took him completely by surprise. It was of no consequence that the charges had little if any foundation. His fate had been decided before the commission set out for Carlisle.

On March 3rd, 1323, Sir Andrew de Harcla was hanged at Harraby and his body drawn and quartered. He died with great fortitude, affirming to the end that his dealings with the King of Scotland had meant no hurt to his own King and country.

With Sir Andrew, the peacemaker, gone the fighting between England and Scotland continued, the Scots attacking Carlisle in 1337, 1345, 1380, 1385 and yet again in 1387.

Although England and Scotland were not at war there was ceaseless hostility immediately north of Carlisle. The border was undefined and came to be known as the Debatable Land. Border clans like the Armstrongs, the Grahams and the Eliots ruled there for the next three hundred years or so. A law unto themselves, they accepted allegiance to neither country. Raiding and plundering indiscriminately both north and south, they shared their nefarious activities with moss troopers and reivers who also inhabited the savage borderland.

By the middle of the 14th century the castle was again falling into disrepair and within the city itself standards of hygiene had fallen so low that a report sent to the King in 1345 informed that "in the city of Carlisle the air is so corrupted and tainted with dung and manure

On the Nunnery Walks
near Kirkoswald
Photo: Walt Unsworth

heaps and so much other filth put in the streets and lanes, and logs are in the said streets and lanes that the common passage is impeded." Several years later, the Black Death struck.

A further charter was granted to Carlisle by Edward III in 1352. It established the city's right to "a free guild and a free election of their mayor and bailiffs." It also granted them the right to hold a Great Fair. This Fair is still proclaimed every August 26th at 8.00am. from the steps of Carlisle Cross.

Henry VII the first of the Tudors, was keen to establish peace and order throughout his kingdom and as a step towards this end he agreed to the marriage of his daughter, Margaret, to James of Scotland. He tried hard to settle the boundary between England and Scotland and proposed that the River Esk should be the boundary of the Debatable Land on the English side. In this he had a limited success and a slender peace did prevail for a few years although clan warfare and borderland raiding continued unabated.

Border ballads telling of this troubled Debatable Land during the hundred and twenty years of Tudor sovereignty are regularly sung today and consequently have become not only well known but well loved.

One of the best known of the narrative poems, Kinmont Willie, brings out all the flavour of those unsettled times. From time to time the Wardens of the Marches on both sides of the border held a trew, a border truce meeting, to allow any particular business to be transacted and on these occasions the spasmodic raiding and pilfering would cease. On one of these truce days, in March 1596, William Armstrong of Kinmont, one of the most notorious of the border "broken-men" or outlaws, was captured while protected by the trew. He was handed over to Mr Salkerd, Lord Scrope's deputy, and shut up in Carlisle castle. Lord Scrope was Warden of the Western Marches of England.

Lord Buccleugh, having failed to parley for Kinmont Willie's release, rode out to rescue him. At dead of night on April 13th, 1596, at the head of a large band of marchmen, he set off to break into Carlisle castle and free his friend. A few of his men were dressed, as he was, as fighting men, a similar number carried ladders like a mason gang, ten looked like hunters and the rest looked like the outlaws they were.

Leaving the Debatable Land for English soil they were soon confronted by Salkerd who demanded to know why they were there. The answers varied: those dressed as hunters said they were looking for an English stag that had trespassed into Scotland; those in the garb of fighting men said they were out to catch a man who had broken faith with Buccleugh; the mason gang said they were going with their ladders to "herry a corbie's nest." When Salkerd questioned the others, their leader, Dickie of Dryhope, did not bother to reply. He simply stuck his lance through the hapless man; and the party rode on.

The Eden, when they reached it, was swollen by heavy rain. Yet without hesitation they rode into the cold flood water and, amazingly, all reached the other bank without mishap. They moved away from the river on foot, head on into the full force of a howling gale. Bodies bent against it and eyes narrowed to mere slits against the slanting, stinging rain, they came to the castle wall.

The first intimation the watchman had that all was not well was when strong fingers circled his neck and squeezed. The strangler flung the limp body to one side and continued his search for Kinmont Willie. Red Rowan found him and carried him to the ladders. Meanwhile Buccleugh, delighted at the way events were moving, shouted his trumpeter to blow his clan's ancient fighting refrain. The trumpeter did so while the challenging words were shouted into the night: "O wha dare meele wi' me?" Gaining bravado from Buccleugh's battle-cry, Kinmont Willie, while being carried down the ladders, shouted derisive insults to Lord Scrope.

Lord Scrope, fearful of losing his prisoner, was in a vile temper. Hurriedly he gathered about him a number of his men and gave chase.

Buccleugh and his men, together with Kinmont Willie, ran back to where they had left their horses near the river and, moving with incredible speed, mounted and spurred them into action. Once more they plunged into the angry, brown waters of the Eden, which was still rising as a consequence of all the rain that had fallen during the previous twenty-four hours and was continuing to fall. Again luck was their friend and they reached the opposite bank without loss.

Lord Scrope and his men reached the river bank just in time to see the stragglers from Buccleugh's party reach the opposite shore. Had the Eden been low or even at its usual depth he would have ridden across it without hesitation. However, the Eden in spate was a different matter. He eyed the fast-flowing current and decided that it would be safer for him to stay where he was. So Kinmont Willie survived to became, once more, a thorn in Lord Scrope's side.

In January 1540, the priory of Carlisle cathedral was dissolved and in May 1541 reformed as the Cathedral Church of the Holy and Undivided Trinity. Lancelot Salkeld, Carlisle's last Roman Catholic prior, became its first Anglican dean.

During the "Pilgrimage of Grace" a northern rising in protest at Henry VIII's ruthless antagonism towards the religious houses, seventy-four protesters were hanged on the city walls as rebels when their protest march on Carlisle failed.

In 1542, when Henry VIII declared war on Scotland, Carlisle became a military headquarters once again. In November of that year, at Solway Moss near Longtown, three thousand English soldiers thoroughly defeated fourteen thousand Scots. An unfortunate side effect of this Scottish defeat was a serious upsurge of pillaging and burning by the lawless clans of the Debatable Land.

For the next decade or so following the death of Henry VIII in 1547 determined efforts were made to introduce law and order into the Debatable Lands through a system of policing. The system worked reasonably well and lawlessness did decrease somewhat during that time.

At the coronation of Elizabeth I as Queen of England in 1558 it was the Bishop of Carlisle, Owen Ogelthorpe who performed the ceremony. This was a great honour for the city which at that time was reorganising its municipal life. In connection with this, a code of by-laws was drawn up and recorded in the Dormant Book. Some of the by-laws dealt with the safety of the city whilst other concerned the keeping clean of the city streets.

The Mayor's Oath, which is set out in the Dormant Book is repeated today by each succeeding mayor on mayor-making day in May. The Dormant Book itself is preserved among the city's archives.

The scandal following the marriage of Mary, Queen of Scots, to the Earl of Bothwell, whom everyone regarded as Darnley's murderer, provoked a rebellion against her and she surrendered at Carberry Hill and abdicated in favour of her son by Darnley, James VI of Scotland. She was imprisoned at Lochleven castle but escaped in May, 1568, was defeated at Langside and fled to England seeking Elizabeth's protection.

Her advisors had written to Sir Richard Lowther, the Deputy Warden of the Marches, to find out if she could be received in friendship at Carlisle. But without waiting for his reply Mary impetuously crossed the Solway and landed at Workington, where, the following day, Sir Richard met her and brought her to Carlisle to await the outcome of Elizabeth's deliberations.

At first Elizabeth, her jealous cousin, was unsure as to how to deal with Mary; but she made it plain to the warden, Lord Scrope, than on no account was she to be allowed to escape.

While awaiting Elizabeth's pleasure Mary lodged in apartments in a tower of the castle, since demolished, and worshipped regularly at the cathedral. In all, she spent six weeks at Carlisle, during which time hunts and other entertainments were arranged for her. She exercised regularly along Ladies Walk where she planted some trees and was generally well cared for. But as the weeks passed, she realised that never again would she enjoy freedom.

The decision to move her from Carlisle came in July, 1569. Mary resisted and Lord Scrope feared that those of Mary's followers who were in Carlisle would come to her aid. However, no such rising materialised and on July 13th she agreed to leave the city and stay, instead, at Lowther castle with Sir Richard Lowther because she saw him as a friend. Her stay there was a short one: only one night, before being taken to Castle Bolton, a further step along the eighteen years long road to her execution at Fotheringhay.

Sir Richard Lowther's genuine affection for Mary did not pass unnoticed. Elizabeth had him consigned to the Tower of London.

Following Queen Elizabeth's death in 1603, James VI of Scotland became James I of England, the first monarch over the two kingdoms, a development which did not impress the Armstrongs, the Grahams and others of their kind who, as ever, held allegiance to none but themselves. The border had now come to be known as "the land of the middleshires" which had about it a friendlier ring than "the Debatable Land". But all else was unchanged and likely to remain that way while "that bloodie and thievish clanne of Armstrongs" and the rest of the free booters, reivers, smugglers, thieves and vagabonds ruled this wild and lawless region.

Almost impenetrable marsh lay to the north of Carlisle while in every other direction moors and open common unfolded into the distance. So dangerous did the city's inhabitants consider their surrounding that few stirred beyond the city walls unless circumstances forced them to do so.

James I, fully aware of their problems appointed a Royal Commission to administer the middle shires. It held its first meeting in Carlisle on April 9th, 1605. When the King came to stay in Carlisle during August, 1617, he visited the cathedral. While there he was reminded by the bishop that the only means of livelihood for the people was fishing and that the city was "in great ruin and extreme poverty." Then several requests were made for assistance but the King did nothing about them.

Charles I, who succeeded James I, granted the city a new charter in 1637 and this is still Carlisle's Governing Charter. One of the privileges it granted was the right to carry the royal sword and maces before the mayor in procession. This gave the citizens the right to govern themselves for the sword is the emblem of civic independence. It is always carried sheathed to denote the reserve of force behind the civil power. The maces carry the arms of England showing that the authority entrusted to the mayor during his year of office is authorised by the Crown.

During the Civil War, Carlisle became the most important Royalist stronghold in the north; and, as such, a prime target for Cromwell's army. Both garrison and citizens knew that it was only a matter of time before the Scots under General Lesley would march against them; and in anticipation they laid in a stock of provisions.

In October, 1644, Lesley advanced on Carlisle with 4,000 Scots but instead of attacking he laid siege to the place. The weeks became months and food supplies began to dwindle. By Christmas all the corn, the cattle and the beer were pooled to be redistributed as weekly rations. To ensure fair play these were paid for by siege coins which had been minted from melted down silver and plate. By mid-summer, 1645, the horses, which had been fed on thatch from the roofs of hovels until they were needed to feed the defenders, had all been eaten. The only remaining sources of food were emaciated dogs and rats. But the defenders refused to surrender.

That summer, on June 23rd and 24th, Lesley sent an emissary to discuss surrender terms with the garrison commander. On both occasions the defenders plied the messenger with the last of their beer, while they drank water and got him so drunk that he reported back that there was still plenty of strong ale to be drunk in the castle. This had the salutary effect of filling Lesley with admiration for them. When, the following day, the articles of surrender were signed the terms offered were more honourable than otherwise would have been the case. The siege had lasted eight months, the longest in Carlisle's history; and the defenders had covered themselves in pride.

In April, 1648, Royalist forces recaptured Carlisle but the Cromwellians snatched it back in September of that year.

The Act of Union of 1707 by which England and Scotland became united in law as well as by sovereign drew many Scots to support the Stuarts; and when, in 1715 an invasion threat reached Carlisle the authorities locked all known papists and other supporters of the Jacobite cause into Carlisle castle. Thus when the Scots crossed into England in October, 1715, few people were willing to rally to them. The rebels avoided Carlisle, proclaimed the Old Pretender James VIII of Scotland at Brampton and Penrith and came to grief at Preston.

When, on November 8th, 1745, the Old Pretender's son, Prince Charles Edward Stuart, crossed the Esk into England determined to restore his father to the British throne, Carlisle was caught with its metaphoric pants down.

The city's defences were poor, the guns obsolete. The garrison consisted of only eighty soldiers, all old and infirm and discipline simply did not exist. A couple of local clergy on the cathedral tower, armed with a huge telescope, acted as lookouts.

On November 9th they spotted about sixty mounted scouts on the Stanwix side of the Eden. The following morning clearing mist revealed the rebels closing in on the city, great numbers of them converging on the three gates. The defenders took up their positions ready for the expected attack. Throughout that day and the following long night they stood at their posts ready to repel an attack which never came. The next morning not one of the enemy could be seen. Disbelief gave way to rejoicing and handshaking; and the deputy-mayor rapturously sent a dispatch to inform the King that the garrison had beaten off the Scottish attack.

The Young Pretender, with most of his army, kept well to the east of Carlisle. On hearing that an English force under General Wade was at Newcastle ready to advance against him, he ordered that the detachment he had sent to capture Carlisle rejoin the main force at Brampton. Hence the sudden withdrawal of the Scots from the city on November 11th.

The old road between Carlisle and Newcastle having fallen into such a ruinous state that moving along it was virtually impossible, General Wade was unable to come to the help of the besieged city. Charles Edward, quick to take advantage of Wade's inability to move his army against him, decided to have another shot at capturing Carlisle. On November 13th the Scots assaulted the city's tottering walls using ladders they had built en route.

It was a bloodless victory. The militia deserted and pandemonium reigned within the city. Everyone clamoured for surrender and eventually the mayor and corporation surrendered the keep to the

Young Pretender at Brampton. On November 17th, Charles Edward Stuart entered Carlisle, heading a parade of his victorious men led by a hundred pipers and proclaimed his father King James VIII of Scotland and James III of England from Carlisle Cross.

Bonnie Prince Charlie remained in Carlisle until November 22nd, when he marched south, leaving only enough men to garrison the castle. Within a month, on December 19th he was back, having got as far south as Derby, dejected, his cause lost and with the Duke of Cumberland breathing down his neck. He remained in Carlisle just long enough to increase the garrison to 400 men to hold up his pursuers, before continuing his retreat back into Scotland.

The Duke of Cumberland - "Butcher" to the Scots and "Sweet William" to the English, who named a flower after him - reached Carlisle on December 21st where, outside the city walls, he awaited the arrival of six eighteen pounders from Whitehaven. They arrived on December 28th, were used to pound the defences all that day and on December 30th, 1745, Carlisle surrendered.

Whilst in Carlisle, the Duke stayed at Highmoor House where Prince Charles had stayed the previous month and slept in the same bed the Prince had used.

The second half of the eighteenth century saw a marked improvement in Carlisle's status. Where in 1759 a visitor described it as "a small, deserted, dirty city, poorly built and poorly inhabited" another in 1773 said "the streets are kept remarkably clean, the principal of which is spacious and contains many modern and elegant houses." Where in 1745 the old road from Carlisle to Newcastle was in so parlous a state General Wade was unable to use it, the one built to replace it between 1751 and 1758 and running for most of its way along the length of Hadrian's Wall is still in excellent condition today and often referred to as the military road. Where, in 1745, life in Carlisle was insular, meagre and fraught with danger and disease, by the last quarter of the 18th century the citizens were beginning to enjoy a fuller, safer standard of living. There were lamps on the main streets, a textile industry had been started, a library had opened and, on October 27th, 1780 the Carlisle Journal began publication. Moreover, the population was growing steadily. From 4,000 in 1763 it had reached 9,500 by 1800.

By 1807 printed cottons, hats, whips and hooks were being manufactured in the city, which also accommodated a soap-boilery, tanners, skinners, three foundries, four breweries and five banks. But weaving was the principal occupation.

Despite the city's general progress, there were serious setbacks. One involved the weavers and fashion caused it. About 1810, ginghams were very popular with the middle and upper classes who purchased them for half a crown a yard. Then fashion changed, the price dropped to 23/4d per yard and the weavers became impoverished. They rioted, through hunger, in 1812, stole and slaughtered sheep for food, broke into potato clamps and flung doors and fences onto bonfires which had been built in the streets for warmth. In 1813 they attacked Denton Mill; but their lot failed to improve. Heartily fed up following six more grim years during which many families had no bread for weeks on end, the weavers voted "to petition the Regent to send us all to America." They thought conditions could not get any worse; and they were wrong. In 1826 they had to face a winter of exceptional severity. To ease their poverty slightly, the weavers were given the task, for a few coppers a day, of building a walk from the castle to the Eden Bridges and this is still called the Weavers Bank.

The population had leaped to 21,000 by 1838, some 17% of which was involved one way or another with weaving. In that year there were 1,963 looms in Carlisle, some in cotton factories but most in the homes of the working people where usually one room was set aside for the loom which was worked by all the family.

For a great many years Carlisle was associated with affairs maritime. Until Whitehaven was developed as one, Carlisle had been Cumberland's major port since Elizabethan times. Between 1825 and 1840 at least half a dozen ships were built in the canal basin. In 1823 the short canal from Carlisle to Port Carlisle was opened and remained in business until August 1853, when it was drained. A railway was built along the canal bed the following year.

It was the coming of the railways that killed the plan to extend the canal to Newcastle. The Newcastle-Carlisle Railway, which was started in 1829 and opened in 1835, ran along exactly the same route as had been planned for the canal.

Throughout the country business men were forsaking canals for railways. The Age of Steam had arrived and Carlisle's involvement was prodigious. By 1876 seven railway companies - the North British; the Caledonian; the Glasgow and South Western; the London and North Western; the Maryport and Carlisle; the North Eastern; the Midland - had their termini at the Citadel Station. The Carlisle-Settle section of the Midland railway, which runs spectacularly along the Eden Valley, was opened on May 1st, 1876.

When, in 1756, Carlisle's first brewery was set up on the River Caldew, a tributary of the Eden, the brewers faced a great deal of prejudice from the locals who were used to brewing their own. Yet by the end of the 18th century this bias had been overcome and four breweries were in production, all near the Caldew. These four breweries served the city and the surrounding area for well over a century, together brewing 18,500 barrels annually. At the beginning of World War I there were 119 licensed houses within the city alone. It was big business.

In 1915 the Ministry of Munitions selected a site near Gretna for a munitions factory. Many navvies employed in its building and, following them, the munition workers were lodged in Carlisle. Highly paid, divorced from a normal home life and other ties, many found solace in drink. Soon convictions for drunkenness in Carlisle rose to almost six times the national average. What was to be done about it? The Central Control Board (Liquor Traffic), seeing that prohibition was not the answer, opted for the State purchase of all except two of Carlisle's licensed premises, the exceptions being the Crown and Mitre Hotel and the County and Station Hotel. To discourage excessive drinking, patrons were discouraged from standing at the bar to drink, snugs were abolished, food was made available and managers were paid a fixed wage rather than any form of commission.

At the top of the Board's list of priorities was the closure of fifty-eight of the licensed houses. This was followed, in 1916, by the take-over of the four breweries and the closure of two of them, the employees being transferred to the remaining two.

In 1912 the Control Board became the Carlisle and District State Management Scheme and was known as such until March 31st 1973, when it was sold off to various independent breweries. Some of the pubs were purchased by breweries as job lots, good and bad houses being lumped together. Others went to private individuals and one of the last to be privatised was the Redfern Inn which, being close to our route, is handy. But there are sixty-six more licensed premises in the city so there is ample choice.

Today Carlisle is a proud manufacturing city, the home of several nationally and internationally known firms like the biscuit people, Carrs of Carlisle, the Metal Box Co. Ltd., makers of a great variety of tin containers, Cowans Sheldon and Co. Ltd., who specialise in harbour, dock-yard and railway installation, the Penguin Confectionery Co. Ltd., home of medicated lozenges and "nipits" and that world renowned civil engineering giant, Laings.

Down the years many famous and interesting people from all walks of life have stayed in proud Carlisle. Doctor Johnson, accompanied by James Boswell, visited the city in 1773. Fifteen years later Boswell became the city's Recorder, a position he held for two years. When Robert Burns stayed at the Malt Shovel Inn in 1773 he chose it because it was the one closest to his beloved Scotland. At that time Burns had a horse called Jenny Geddes and was fined for allowing it to trespass on Corporation grass. Romance came to St. Mary's church, then the cathedral nave, on Christmas Eve, 1797, when Sir Walter Scott married Charlotte Carpenter in that historic building.

Dorothy and William Wordsworth and their great friend Coleridge were in Carlisle on August 16th, 1803, when they "walked upon the city walls which are broken down in places and crumbling away and most disgusting from filth."

Charles Dickens found Carlisle "congenially and delightfully idle" except on market morning when "Carlisle woke up amazingly and became disagreeably and reproachfully busy." That is how he described it in 1857.

May 17th and 18th, 1917, were red letter days for Carlisle because they saw the first official visit of a ruling monarch since 1617 when King George V and Queen Mary paid an informal and semi-private visit to Cumberland. On Edenside the King inspected the Cumberland Volunteer Regiment and chatted with munition workers.

In 1918 the President of the United States, Woodrow Wilson, made a "Pilgrimage of the heart" to Carlisle, birthplace of his mother in 1826.

On May 23rd, 1947, Field-Marshall Viscount Montgomery, whose contribution to the successful outcome of World War II was so outstanding, was made a Freeman of the city.

Today the B.B.C. is well established in Carlisle. Radio Carlisle takes good care of the spoken word while B.B.C. North West is the T.V. outlet. Border T.V. is also well established in the city, providing a very exciting, highly professional alternative channel.

Spreading the news through the printed word began in 1815 when the Carlisle Patriot started publication. In 1865 the paper was taken over by the Carlisle Conservative Newspaper Co. and had its name changed to the Cumberland News in 1910. In 1968 it took over the Carlisle Journal and today is published weekly. Its sister paper, the Evening News and Star is published every evening.

Despite Carlisle's age the armorial bearings of the city are quite recent. In fact they were drawn up, registered and recorded by Letters Patent in September, 1924. The earliest Arms date back to 1462 and show a red cross on a golden field with four red roses and a central fifth rose in gold. A new shield was adopted in 1835 when the Municipal Corporation Act became law. It showed a castle with, above it, the passant lion of England and with wavy lines underneath. In heraldic terms a castle indicates a city and wavy lines a river. The shield represents an English city on the banks of a river. In 1885 this second shield was replaced by a new armorial device which combined both the previous Arms side by side. This would have been the City Arms today had the City Council not been informed, in 1923, that they had never been officially registered. The design had no authority.

The Arms in use today show the original shield with its red cross on a golden field with the four red and one golden roses surmounted by a mural crown showing that Carlisle was once a walled city. A red wyvern or two legged dragon with a forked tail, with golden roses - either four or six and both are equally correct - on its wings stands on either side of the shield, the whole Arms standing on a green mount. The wyverns represent the link between the Celts of Cumbria and Wales.

The original mayoral badge and chain dates from October 10th, 1850, when the then mayor of Carlisle met Queen Victoria's mother, the Duchess of Kent, who was breaking her journey at Carlisle station. In 1898 a new chain and badge, carrying the unauthorised Arms of two shields was purchased and is the one used today.

As the Corporation's responsibilities developed and diversified through the 19th century, various departments were set up around the city centre, mainly in Fisher Street. The Council and its committees met in the Town Hall. All this changed when, on March 12th, 1964, the new, eleven story Civic Centre was opened at the bottom of Rickergate. This modern office block has at first floor level a civic suite which leads to an octagonal council chamber; and it is there that today's Council and officers sit in a circle facing the mayor and conduct civic business in congenial surroundings.

Industry is investing heavily in and around Carlisle and with good reason. For this thriving, picturesque city has became an important communications centre, being superbly served by road, rail and air. Furthermore the public sector has matched private industry with investment in recent years to such an extent that Carlisle has become a worthy capital of England's most beautiful region, Cumbria.

In 1985 its prestigious Lanes Shopping Centre was voted the best in Great Britain and its excellent Sands Centre sports and arts complex on the banks of England's most beautiful river attracts many business people because its facilities for conferences and exhibitions are first rate. The centre also promotes a variety of professional entertainment, catering for all tastes, high and low brows alike.

Carlisle, which had an uneasy birth and a rough upbringing had defied the odds by developing into a capital city, an ugly duckling that has became a swan.

* * *

Justifiably proud of its history and architecture, Carlisle City Council has produced an exciting, informal guide to that part of the city centre between the castle and the market square which covers about three quarters of a mile and takes on average three quarters of an hour to complete. Beginning and ending at the old Town Hall, the trail explores the old walled city around the cathedral precinct. En route it passes among other interesting places, the market cross, the guild hall, St. Cuthbert's church, the 18th century Sportsman Inn, the tithe barn, the cathedral, the Sallyport Steps, which were one of a number of secret gateways in the wall, and the 17th century Tullie House, which houses Carlisle's museum and art gallery. At the northern end of Castle Street an optional detour takes the visitor to the castle which houses Cumbria's Military Museum.

A footpath skirting the northern side of the castle is part of the popular Eden Riverside Trail, another adventurous product of the positive forward looking City Council. The usual starting point is at the southern end of Eden Bridge where, just beyond the abutment, old wooden stumps stick out of the water among a jumble of large, sandstone blocks, the remains of a temporary bridge built after the Eden changed course in 1571. Before that date it flowed in a wide sweep close to the castle. Then, in January 1571, flooding caused a breach in the river bank, shortening this sweep and forming a stream called the Priest Beck. Wooden bridges crossed both the Eden and the beck; but by 1601 they were "in great decay." Two stone bridges replaced them, the cost being stood by the county because at that time this spot was not part of the city. Gradually the channels changed in importance until by the beginning of the 19th century the Priest Beck had became wider than the main channel. The original channel was filled in and the name Priest Beck dropped. Today, although only one bridge crosses the river at this point, local people frequently refer to it as "the Eden bridges."

The Trail is in three stages, the main one, the shortest, keeping close to both sides of the river, the second covering a slightly larger area and the third one almost doubling the distance taken by stage 1. The City Council has published an informative booklet, The Eden Riverside Trail, which is designed to stimulate interest in the Trail. I thoroughly recommend it to all who would like to avail themselves of this splendid facility.

It is sometimes possible to follow the neglected path along the foot of Etterby Scaur. Usually the path is just above the level of the river; but whenever the Eden is in spate it is many feet under water. Thus, frequently the decision to walk it is the river's, not yours. "Walk" is perhaps not the right word for with several large trees lying across our route, parts of which had been washed away, it was more of a scramble. Landslip caused by flood water was an added hazard, but, with care, this dilapidated route is usable. It is hoped, the Authorities told me, that once the problems of landslip have been overcome, this old and very exciting section of river bank can be returned to its original good order, thus opening up a very interesting stretch of water.

This section of the walk is by far the shortest and can be completed in an hour. But if you include the Eden Riverside Trail, the Town Centre Trail and the Lanes Shopping Centre this will take much longer. And if you decide to go to the races or play a little golf or do some fishing this will take longer still. By taking advantage of the superb tours on offer which explore the beautiful countryside around Carlisle and include the Lake District and the romantic Borderlands you'd better arrange to stay for a fortnight at least.

Rock carvings by William Mounsey on the sandstone cliffs of the Eden gorge, near Armathwaite

Long Meg and her Daughter
The Eden Way between Sandford and Warcop. Sandford in the background.

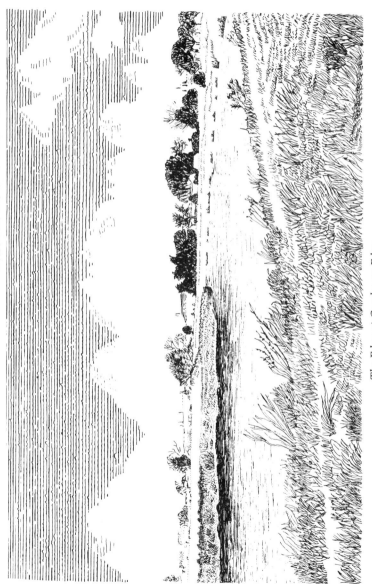

The Eden at Crosby on Eden

3:   Carlisle to Wetheral

Length of section:	9 miles
Total distance:	17 miles
Map:	O.S. Landranger 85 and 86
Handy hostelries:	Fantails, The Crown Hotel, The Wheatsheaf, The Queen Inn.

Route Directions

From the eastern exit of Rickerby Park walk towards the Eden along a path close to the boundary of Rickerby school and with Brunstock Beck on your left. Continue along the path as it curves with the school boundary, parallel to the river and pass the school playing-fields on your left to join a track with houses on either side. Follow the enclosed track, passing two others leading off at right angles on your left and where it bifurcates take the right-hand fork which leads to a small wood. Alternatively, having taken the path from Rickerby Park exit down to the river, continue along the river's edge to where, at the aforesaid small wood, Rickerby Rocks are to be found.

The way is now upstream, following the river bank which at this point makes a huge loop, or, if you prefer, you can avoid this loop by walking due east from the small wood to rejoin the river downstream of the M6 motorway bridge, and, keeping close to the river, follow its bends past Linstock to Park Broom where the way ahead is signposted. Between the motorway bridge and Park Broom there is no public right of way but the owner of the land, Mr Wannup of Linstock House, very kindly allows people to walk across it provided they do no damage and obey the country code.

In times of flood, when the way under the M6 bridge is impassable, turn left away from the river and walk parallel to the M6 to where the road from Rickerby Park to Linstock bars your way. Join it and turn right along it over the motorway. Then cut down the field on your right, keeping close to the M6 on your right, back to the river, on course again having made your necessary detour.

Back on a public footpath at Park Broom, continue upstream for much of the way between the river and the flood barrier, to where the route is blocked by the River Gelt flowing into the Eden. Turn left,

Carlisle to Wetheral

CARLISLE

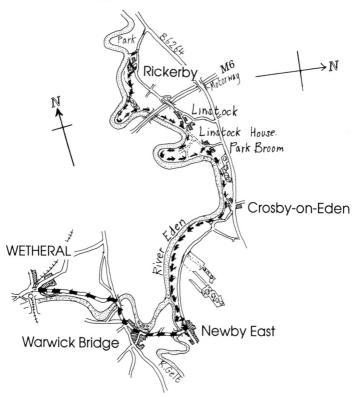

Rickerby

M6 Motorway

Park

B6264

Linstock

Linstock House.

Park Broom

Crosby-on-Eden

River Eden

WETHERAL

Newby East

Warwick Bridge

R. Gelt

N

N

under a line of power lines, along a track and through a field gate onto a minor road.

Turn right along it to nearby Newby East and at a T junction in the hamlet turn right, downhill, and follow the road to Warwick Bridge. Cross the Eden and turn left along the road which for most of its way runs parallel to and alongside the Eden. Where it curves slightly away from the river and climbs steeply take the minor road on your left which leads under Wetheral viaduct. There, climb the 91 steps and take a short, narrow road, past the Crown, to Wetheral village green and the end of the section.

The Background Story

Meandering through middle age the Eden runs deep. Now and then, as at Linstock Rocks, sandstone bedrock pushes close to the surface and sometimes above it. But for the most part the river snakes across the Cumberland Plain with little to ripple its smooth surface. For almost the whole of its length from the Solway, across the Cumberland Plain and up the Eden Valley the river has a sandstone bed. The rich red soil of the low lying meadows through which the river twists on its approach to Carlisle is the result of alluvium deposited when the whole area was a vast flood plain. In season, these water meadows are freckled with wild flowers, and birds in great variety are attracted to them. During the winter months, when those parts not protected by flood barriers lie under water, large flocks of wildfowl use them for feeding.

Some expensive houses smile on Rickerby Park from Carlisle's northern environs while across the Eden, beyond the golf course, the city falls away to southwards, so the retrospective views on moving up river give little hint of a nearby metropolis. The civic centre is clearly seen, as is the older G.P.O. repeater station with its conglomeration of discs; and that's about it. The rest of the city manages to keep a pretty low profile.

How good it is to find that on leaving the park, you are in open country straight away!

Eden Secondary School is a pleasantly sited cluster of fine buildings which seem to embrace all those requirements for scholastic pursuits. It exudes harmony and quietude, so essential for healthy study, has a pleasant playing-field and is far enough removed from heavy traffic and other noisy distractions of a modern city to make other less well endowed schools envious of it. Yet it is under threat of closure because, it appears, there are not enough pupils to make it viable. Shame.

Downstream of where the M6 sweeps across it, the Eden describes a horseshoe. Anyone walking upstream on the northern bank, could take a short cut across the base of this horseshoe, leaving the river soon after passing through a copse and rejoining it where a stile crosses a wire fence near the motorway bridge. But for the purist there is only one way to go - around the horseshoe.

The Eden is one of England's earliest salmon rivers. Salmon fishing started to develop into a sport, as opposed to being primarily a method of acquiring food, by the beginning of the 17th century when the earliest books on how to master the craft of angling began to appear. But it was not until the beginning of Queen Victoria's reign, 1837, that the salmon fisherman became recognised as such in his own right.

It was Izaac Walton who wrote, "Angling may be said to be like the mathematics that it can never fully be learnt." But people do not fish the Eden in order to involve themselves with mathematical problems. They do so, as Richard Waddington observed in 1959, because "salmon fishing is a game which a man and a fish must play together. And while a man can dictate the terms on which the sport shall be enjoyed, he sometimes forgets that the fish has absolute power of veto."

Happily, while most of the English rivers emptying into the North Sea are salmonless, salmon still run up the Eden and other western flowing rivers in almost the same quantities as they have done for years. Nevertheless its future is in jeopardy because generally the species is diminishing. The great age of salmon fishing was from about 1880 to 1930.

Although salmon can be caught in many ways the correct one is with fly. The prominent Victorian salmon fisher, George Kelson, used huge green heart rods, Alexander Grant designed the famous Grant vibration rod and invented a method of fishing with a floating line called the "oiled-line" technique. Percy Laming experimented with small rods and lighter lines. He developed a technique of fishing near the surface by swinging the line around the front of the salmon's nose. He called this method the controlled drag. A.H.E.Wood, acknowledged "father" of modern salmon fishing with a floating line, pioneered what he called the "greased line" technique. This was based on observing that salmon will move further to the fly in summer conditions and are more susceptible to a smaller pattern than they are in the spring.

Salmon fishing requires an extraordinary degree of skill. If the water is right and the fish are there the element of luck plays an important part. But it takes more than luck and dangling brightly coloured feathers in front of a salmon's nose to catch it. When conditions are right most anglers should be able to catch a few salmon; but it takes an expert to catch salmon throughout the season. An ordinary fisher should be able to catch three or four fish on a good day when the river is settling down after spate and a new run has entered the river. But when the water is low he can expect to catch very little.

From Linstock, which stands back from the outside edge of a very tight bend there are good, clear views upstream, downstream and across the river to where, on the far bank an ox-bow is being formed. Because of its elevated position flooding is never a problem, but upstream of the hamlet, where the ground falls away to the flood plain, retaining walls protect the surrounding low lying land. Almost a mile long, the retaining walls curl around the inside of the next bend, stop at the downstream end of an adjoining straight section and continue at intervals for almost as far as the confluence with the lovely River Gelt.

Linstock soil is alluvial on a clay subsoil with a sandy bottom and on it was grown the flax from which the name Linstock if derived. Much of the crop was carted to Wetheral where womenfolk spun it into cloth. It was a monotonous task which they eased by taking their spinning-wheels to neighbours houses where they gossiped and sang while they worked.

A thick walled, sandstone donjon, now a comfortable farmhouse, is all that remains of Linstock castle. The actual date of its erection is uncertain but it was there when Henry I granted Linstock to his chaplain who gave it to the prior and convent of Carlisle. Following the creation of the see, the bishop and convent held their lands in common until a partition was made by the papal legate under which, along with other manors, Linstock was appropriated to the Bishop of Carlisle. For a long time thereafter it was his only seat.

In 1292 Bishop Irton died at the castle and the following year Bishop Halton entertained Johannes Romanus and his 300 strong suite. Entertainment peaked there in 1307 when, between March 6th and 12th, Edward Longshanks stayed at the castle with his queen, Margaret of France, and his court, before moving to Carlisle.

The Bishop of Carlisle is lord of the manor of Linstock which includes the parish of Crosby-on-Eden and has Carlisle airport on its doorstep.

A footpath leads north-east from the river to nearby Crosby-on-Eden, a mix of old and new houses set on both sides of the old military road built by General Wade to facilitate troop movements between Newcastle and Carlisle. The name "Crosby" stems from the ancient cross that once stood on the little hill where Crosby church now stands.

Close to Crosby and just to the north-east of the village is Carlisle airport.

From now on, almost until the River Gelt enters the Eden, the walking is along a level river bank with a flood retaining embankment a few feet away to the left. Behind, the Cumberland plain stretches into the distance. Ahead, a gap in the rising ground increasingly holds our interest. The whole aspect of the river is changing in a most dramatic and exciting way.

Like the Eden into which it flows, the Gelt is a lovely river which meanders through a pastoral, hilly countryside patchworked with woods and well husbanded fields. Two becks, Old Water and New Water, merge below steep sided Tarnmonath Fell to become the Gelt and other feeders swell its clear waters.

Just north of Warwick Bridge, immediately upstream of its confluence with the Gelt, the Eden frees itself from the confines of the Eden Valley proper. As for Warwick Bridge itself, it is pleasantly sited at a point on the river where it is spanned by a fine stone, three arched bridge. The bridge was built in 1837 by John Dobson of Newcastle and today it carries the busy A69. This road separates the village from its church which is built in the old Norman style and dedicated to St. Leonard. Warwick, which means "the dwelling on the bank" is built on a rich and fertile soil consisting principally of sandy loam.

On an eminence near the bridge are the remains of an earthwork thought to have been built to guard the river in moss-trooper days.

Peter Dixon was mayor of Carlisle in 1837-38. He owned a cotton mill in the city which at that time was the largest in England. In 1840, he commissioned the same John Dobson who had been responsible for the construction of Warwick Bridge to build him a fine home worthy of his station in life. Holme Eden Hall, on the river's eastern bank, was the result. Until recently it was occupied by an enclosed Order of Benedictine nuns and today is an old folks' home. When the nuns moved out, all the headstones of their departed were removed to a little churchyard on a hill near the Haywain pub in Little Corby, overlooking a beck. At least it looks like a beck but really it is neither beck nor stream. It is a river as sure as the Eden into which it flows is a river. The locals will not have it any other way.

Warwick Hall, on the other side of the River Eden, is not what it used to be. The original hall with its strong Jacobite associations was rebuilt in 1828 and again in 1936 following a serious fire.

During his stay at Brampton, Bonnie Prince Charlie was entertained at Warwick Hall, at that time the home of a staunch Roman Catholic family. When, on November 13th, 1745, the Jacobite army mustered to march on Carlisle, Warwick Bridge was the site. On November 17th, the Young Pretender, riding his white horse, rode out from Warwick Bridge to take over the city.

Many of the scaling ladders taken by the Jacobite troops to Carlisle were made from branches gathered in the area. Some came from Warwick Hall and others from Great Corby and the grounds of Corby castle.

Great Corby, which means "Core's settlement" with the "by" showing its Old Swedish link, stands high above the Eden on its right bank a good mile upstream of Warwick Bridge. It is a very pleasant village, quite large and has some very attractive houses. The reading room dates from 1877 when it was built by public subscription. It is now used as the village hall. Close to its door is the 1914-18 war memorial tablet. There has been a school in Great Corby since 1720 and a Methodist chapel since 1889. The enclosed common tends to be cold and wet, otherwise the soil is a good mix of sand and loam.

Was ever an elegant mansion set more gloriously than Corby

castle? This beautiful seat of the Howards, a distinguished branch of the illustrious house of Norfolk, is elegantly situated on top of a steep, wooded bank overlooking the Eden. The surrounding countryside is all harmony and enchantment with rolling hills becoming "bosom'd high in Nature's sylvan majesty" on their precipitous descent to the fish-fat river. It is, indeed, a delightful locality, a most romantic spot, a place for chasing gilded shadows. Castle and grounds are open to the public at a small charge.

There was an 11th century castle, probably a wooden one, standing on the site of today's mansion. This was replaced by a stone pele tower which, in turn, was enclosed within the present building during the 13th and 14th centuries.

The manor of Corby was granted by Henry II to Hubert de Vaux who gave it to Odard whose posterity assumed the name of De Corby or Corby. During the reign of Edward I it came into the family of Richmond who conveyed it to the Earl of Carlisle, Andrew de Harcla, who by now had become one of England's premier earls.

Harcla entered into a peace treaty with Robert Bruce, King of Scots. He sent a copy of the treaty to Edward II who, following a disastrous end to a ruthless and sadistic campaign against the Scottish rebels, had fled to Yorkshire. The King reacted with great suspicion to the treaty and sent Anthony de Lucy to Cockermouth to arrest Harcla. The Earl was not at Cockermouth: he was in Carlisle castle, busy with his normal administrative duties. When arrested he offered no resistance. He was condemned without trial and, on March 3rd, 1323, was executed in Carlisle for treason, by the same King he had served so well and who, a brief year earlier had ennobled him. It had been Richard Salkeld who had arrested Harcla and "for his good services in taking Andrew de Harcla, Earl of Carlisle, prisoner" - was given Corby castle in 1335.

In 1624 Lord William Howard of Naworth, the man who did so much to bring peace to the border, bought the castle for his son, Sir Francis Howard and it has been in the family ever since.

Using rich, red sandstone hewn at a quarry in the grounds, Henry Howard entirely remodelled the castle, creating today's beautiful Georgian mansion. The work, which was begun about 1809, took several years to complete. The facade is classical and it has a fine Doric front. A lion stantant guardant, the crest of the Howards, menaces the visitors from a pedestal in the centre of the parapet. At midnight on every New Year's Eve, so the story goes, the lion wags its tail!

The romantic walks which hug the river for about a mile are an early example of naturalistic landscaping. Commissioned by Thomas Howard early in the 18th century, they weave most delightfully through an exquisite sylvan area bedecked with classical statuary. There is a summer-house decorated with sculptures, a temple which used to house musical entertainments, a statue of St. Constantine looking across the river to St. Constantine's Cells and another, a huge one, representing Polyphemus overlooking one of the paths. Locals call it "Belted Will," the nickname given to William Howard. But the piece de resistance is the Cascade which was built to give a fall of 100 feet into a basin with a fountain, the water pouring from the mouths of seven weird creatures. The central one is large with prominent eyes, the rest of it being mainly mouth and teeth. On each side of it are three identical miniatures. After the Battle of Trafalgar the fountain at the foot of the Cascade was replaced by a statue of Nelson. Thomas Howard liked to entice unsuspecting guests into the caves behind the Cascade then open the sluices. The ensuing curtain of water was then supposed to trap them; but since the water supply stream was often dry, the joke simply failed to work.

To saunter in such evocative surroundings is like stepping into the 18th century. You half expect to meet splendidly attired gentlemen with silk stockings on their legs and silver buckles on their shoes, strutting proud as peacocks and doffing tricorn hats with a flamboyant sweep of the arm while bending low and making gay leg to elegantly coiffured, richly brocaded ladies.

Just as Thomas Howard was a pioneer of early landscaping, so Philip Howard was a pioneer agriculturalist. He was the first landowner in Cumberland to introduce turnips and clover to that county.

The noble pile of Corby castle makes a fitting seat for a branch of a family with as impeccable a pedigree as the Howards, who are descended in direct line from King Edward I.

"The banks of the River Eden about Corby are worthy of notice both on account of their natural beauty and the viaducts which have recently been carried over the bed of the river and over a neighbouring ravine." So noted William Wordsworth. The one over the Eden, Wetheral viaduct, was built between 1830 and 1833 to carry the old North Eastern Railway from Carlisle to Newcastle. Most of the sandstone used in its construction came from a quarry at Newbiggin and the filling from an adjacent quarry, which is now a bowling green. Although the structure is huge, 625 feet long and 99 feet high with five semi-circular arches, each 80 feet wide, it does not look out of place, thanks to the rich red sandstone facing which blends so beautifully with the red sandstone cliffs at either side of the river. The views it commands on either side are magnificent and well worth the walk along the iron footbridge.

Were it not for the footbridge, residents of Corby and Wetheral would be obliged to cross the Eden either by making a detour by Warwick Bridge, using the ferry, which operated until the mid-1950s, or, if the river was low enough by making use of the ford, or Monk's Wath, slightly downstream of the viaduct. Once subject to a toll of $1/2$d, which British Rail raised to 1d, crossing the bridge is now free.

On the opposite, upstream, side of the viaduct there is an iron railing which at first extended part of the way across the viaduct from Wetheral station and was later extended to the other side. It was placed there as a safeguard following a fatal accident.

Not everyone welcomed the coming of the railways, especially Sunday traffic which was thought to be ungodly. One clergyman, shocked at the prospect of a Sunday trip from Carlisle to Newcastle, distributed a notice which read:-

REWARD FOR SABBATH BREAKING
"People taken safely and swiftly to Hell next Lord's Day by the Carlisle Railway for 7/6.
It is a Pleasure Trip."

It was, indeed, a pleasure trip and perhaps to some of the passengers Newcastle's mean back streets may have looked like the gateway to Hell. But the countryside through which the line passed, particularly in the vicinity of Wetheral, was like the breath of Heaven.

A fine approach to Wetheral is along the pleasant road from Warwick Bridge which keeps close to the river's left bank and gives the walker his or her first glimpse of the sheer magnificence of the scenery of this glorious part of the Eden Valley.

Where the road begins to swing slightly away from the river to climb the hill with Wetheral perched on top, continue straight ahead on a level, minor road edging the river to the left. It enters a ravine, a most delightful one, whose banks are clothed with hanging woods which are breathtaking when autumn tints appear. Beyond the ancient ford the viaduct in all its red splendour holds the eye. What a grand structure it is! How well it blends with the river scenery, which thereabouts has no equal in all England!

On the right, a flight of steps has been cut into the steep ravine side close to the viaduct. Known locally as the "91 steps," each tread is a solid stone sleeper removed from the railway track when wooden sleepers were introduced.

Between Wetheral and Armathwaite

4:   Wetheral to Armathwaite

Length of section:	8 miles
Total distance:	25 miles
Map:	O.S. Landranger 86
Handy hostelries:	The Duke's Head,
	The Fox and Pheasant

Route Directions

Leave Wetheral green by the south-east corner, below the cross, and take the road downhill, passing the parish church, to the river. There turn right and go along the river bank to a flight of stone steps, which climb. Continue along the path ahead to Wetheral Woods, which enter through a kissing gate. Go along the clear path through the woods which climbs to pass St. Constantine's Cells, then drops back to river level.

On leaving the woods keep to the river bank until Wetheral pumping station on the right, is passed, when take the broad farm track up Primrose Bank as far as a gate across it with Cote House Farm on the right just beyond it. Go through the gate and immediately turn left, cross a stile and follow the markers through a shallow wood, downhill to rejoin the river at a point where there is a large island in the middle of it. Now follow the river's edge upstream, passing Cote House Tower Farm on your right, set back at the bottom of a steep hillside.

Cross a stile leading into a small wood, pass Matthew Knublay's tombstone and follow the path until it begins to curve away from the river where go left and, keeping close to the river continue upstream through pastures. There is no defined path but you have right of way.

Continue along the river bank, first crossing a pasture, then going through a wood along a defined path, then crossing a longer pasture to enter another, longer wood at a point where there is another large island in the river.

At the end of this long wood, where a signpost points uphill on the right, cross a stile straight ahead and, following markers, aim for the field to the right of a narrow wood which edges the river. The marked

<u>Wetheral to Armathwaite</u>

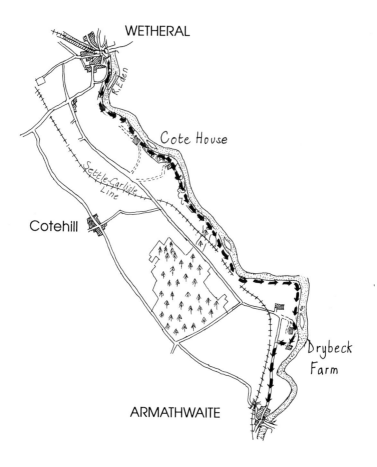

WETHERAL

R. Eden

Cote House

Settle Carlisle Line

Cotehill

Drybeck Farm

ARMATHWAITE

63

Matthew Knublay's tombstone

way climbs uphill, then levels off, keeping close to the wood on its left. At the end of the wood turn left and return downhill to the river.

Continue upstream, walking in an easterly direction across open pasture to where the river bends to due south. Still keeping close to the river follow the clear path ahead to join a farm road which leads past Drybeck Farm, away from the river to the Wetheral to Armathwaite road. Turn left along it for just over a mile to Armathwaite and the end of the section.

The Background Story
Like good wine, Wetheral, the beautiful Cumbrian village with the Anglo Saxon name meaning "the haugh or steep grassy bank where sheep are kept," has improved with age; and it always was a lovely spot. In the third century a small community lived there close to the edge of Inglewood Forest, once the largest hunting preserve in England.

The Angles expanding westwards from their Northumbrian Kingdom, settled there during the 7th century and for most of the 10th and 11th centuries it was part of the Scottish Kingdom of Strathclyde.

When William II, Rufus, succeeded the Crown in 1087 he determined to settle his northern border. To this end he seized the southern part of Cumbria and began to rebuild Carlisle which had lain ruinous for 200 years. He also made the Solway the north-west boundary of his Kingdom and gave the lordship of this district to Ranulf de Meschin, one of his most trusted Norman barons, who had his headquarters at Appleby.

Ranulf de Meschin gave the manor of Wetheral to the Benedictine Abbey of St. Mary, York, as endowment. With characteristic Norman efficiency he picked a superb site for the monastery on a hillside overlooking the Eden. The mother house sent a prior and twelve monks to set up the monastery, which extended from the present gateway to the river's edge. Within the priory walls there was a church, a guest house and a hospital. Local villagers were given employment working the mill-bay and the salmon sluices and tilling the land.

Ranulf de Meschin took good care to ensure that the salmon sluices and the mill-bay were secured to the priory monks by a separate charter. Neither the fish nor the water on either side of the river below the large pool at the bottom of the priory as far as the Monkswath had to be disturbed. This was very important because the salmon caught in the coops placed there made a valuable contribution to the priory's kitchen. The Lord of Crosby to whom the sluices and the fishing had once belonged before they became part of the priory's endowment, received every eighth fish taken.

Others added grants and rich endowments to those made by Ranulf de Meschin and these were confirmed by Henry I who also granted pannage for swine without payment of the usual forest dues. Succeeding kings added more privileges and immunities to this important cell of the Abbey of St. Mary's, which now provided vicars and chaplains for Wetheral church and the chapel at Warwick and saw to their upkeep and maintenance. So the priory prospered, as did the villagers who were taught about religion, healing and agriculture and continued to be employed in and about the priory buildings, the mill and the fishing.

In return for these benefits the villagers were expected to fulfil certain services to the priory. These included each tenant carrying the priory corn in the autumn, one reaper and one ploughman working for the prior on one day annually, tenants carrying wood for the fishgate and the mill, effecting repairs to the mill and the weir and paying a thirteenth portion of the corn ground there for mulcture.

The priory was a place of sanctuary, a privilege granted to it by Henry I in his Charter of Rights. Six gryth crosses marked the boundaries of the sanctuary but time has erased the situation of all but one. The word gryth is Anglo Saxon and means peace.

Sanctuary could be claimed by anyone who had committed murder "suddenly without enmity" or "without laying at wait" through fleeing to the Liberty at Wetheral and, by old custom, claiming gryth by ringing the bell in church and swearing before the bailiff of the Liberty that they would in future conduct themselves well and faithfully. They could then live in peace within the Liberty but must not go outside the boundary.

Following the Dissolution of the Monasteries possession of the priory was granted to the Dean and Chapter of Carlisle. At the time of the Commonwealth the Manor of Wetheral was sold by their commissioners to Richard Banks of Cockermouth but on the restoration of the monarchy the Dean and Chapter recovered their property.

All that remains of the priory is the gatehouse. It now belongs to the National Trust which has done some superb restoration work on it.

Wetheral church with its ancient churchyard stands in a dip in the hillside within sight of and close to the priory. It is thought that an earlier Anglo Saxon church once stood on the same site but no trace of it remains. To marauding Scots nothing was sacred and they constantly attacked Wetheral and its church because the village was sited in Inglewood Forest, which they considered to belong to their King.

The church Ranulf de Meschin gave to the Abbey of St. Mary's at York probably had only a nave and a chancel, the aisles being added at a later date. The layout of the church, apart from the tower, which was built in 1760, is much as it was in the 14th century.

At the western end of the chancel's south wall there is an inscription on the arch which reads, "Orate proaia Willemi Thornton Abbatis." Translated from the Latin it asks anyone to "pray for the soul of William Thornton, Abbot." He was head of the priory circa 1500 and was succeeded as prior in 1530 by Richard Wedderhall for whose

Lych gate, Wetheral church

soul a similar Latin inscription was placed over the priest's door.

A square tower with an outside stairway was added to the church in 1760. The stairway led to an internal gallery where the parish clerk would read out notices of local events in the days before cheap printing and the introduction of the penny post. This tower was replaced by the present one in 1882.

Attached to the north side of the chancel is the Howard chapel, built in 1791, above the 13th century mausoleum of the Howard family of Corby castle. Twenty-five members of the Howard family are thought to be interred in this vault which was first used in 1663 when Mary, second wife of Sir Francis Howard was laid to rest there. The last person to be consigned to the vault was Philip, elder son of Henry Howard, in 1882, when it was finally sealed off.

The red sandstone chapel itself was built to house a beautiful white marble statue as a memorial to the young wife of Henry Howard, Maria, who died of childbirth together with her baby daughter in November, 1789, aged only twenty-two. Maria was the daughter and co-heiress of Andrew, Lord Archer, of Umberstade in Warwickshire, and had married Henry Howard just one year earlier, on November

22nd, 1788.

Joseph Nollekens R.A. (1732-1823), an English sculptor whose reputation, in particular for lifelike busts, almost equalled that of Reynolds in painting, was commissioned to do the work. Henry Howard paid him £1,500 for the statue which shows a draped figure, "Faith," pointing upwards with her right hand whilst supporting the head of the dying mother with the other. The mother's dead baby is lying across her lap. This fine group is considered to be Nollekens's greatest work. A grasping man, whose miserliness was exceeded only by that of his wife, Nollekens is said to have burst into tears when he heard where his masterpiece was to be placed because he thought that it would be seen by so few people.

The green, a good-sized, triangular one that falls away sharply at its south-eastern corner, does a tremendous job of opening up the village and so enhancing its beauty.

When under the Inglewood Forest Enclosure Act of 1806 the Commissioners sold off miscellaneous areas of waste land, the piece which was to become Wetheral village green came under the hammer at Penrith. A deputation of villagers was dispatched to the sale with the instructions to purchase it as cheaply as possible. The bidding began to waver and finally stop when they made their call for £30. They thought it was theirs and that they had got a bargain. But before the auctioneer could knock it down to them one of their own party, worse for drink, raised the bidding again and before the others could quieten him the selling price had risen to £60! It was purchased at that price by the villagers, who doubtless had something to say to their colleague later!.

Before being purchased by the villagers this piece of common land was grazed by sheep, goats, pigs and geese, but once the common had become the green all sorts of rules and regulations were applied to it. Children and teenagers had full use of it as a play area, but now no washing was to be dried or bleached on it, no mats or dirt retaining materials were to be shaken there, nor any fire lit and no animals could be grazed there any more. These were the new rules and had to be obeyed; but geese cannot read and they continued to eat away at it until it was "nearly as bare as the road."

The village pump at the south-west corner of the common, close to a carpenter's workshop, became a regular meeting place for the womenfolk who enlivened their water-gathering with a good gossip.

At the opposite end of the green there were a tithe barn and an ancient inn with a sanded stone floor and a "hallen," which protected drinkers from cold draughts each time someone came into or left the inn while they sank draughts of the local brew.

Local grown flax which had been "beetled" or pummelled to soften the tissues on beetling stones in the river, hackled, carded and spun by the womenfolk was woven into linen in a weaving shed sited at the south-eastern end of the green; and very good quality linen it was too: far superior to any brought into Wetheral from other areas.

In 1814 a maypole, generously donated by Mr Howard of Corby castle, was erected in the middle of the green. It was a larch tree, dressed and painted and topped with a weather-cock that turned out to be too heavy for it. Once this was realised, the weather-cock was removed and put on the church tower where it remained until the tower was demolished in 1882. Circa 1845 the maypole was removed from the middle of the green so that it would not interfere with the children's games. It was re-sited at the green's south-east corner. This transfer took place on a summer evening and there were many willing helpers because a cask of ale had been opened to regale the thirsty workers. That same evening and at the very same time as the maypole was being taken down, a lecturer, at the other end of the green, was giving a talk on the evil of intoxicating liquor. His intentions were good but his audience was a very poor one, especially while the cask of ale lasted.

The stone cross which today stands on the village green is the one that replaced the maypole, which was becoming unsafe. Again, Mr Howard was the benefactor.

In the middle of the 18th century a strange looking building with two six-sided, crenellated towers was built on the edge of Wetheral by the five spinster daughters of Dr Waugh, Chancellor of Carlisle. It stood on the edge of the wood, not far from the priory, overlooking the Eden; and the views, on every side were magnificent. During the time the five misses Waugh lived in "The Folly" as this strange house came to be known, they became well known for their charity and respected for their piety. No trace of "The Folly" remains but in the field between it and the village faint traces of the old strip farming days can still be seen.

To the right, on leaving the south end of Wetheral along the road to Wetheral Pasture a group of trees on raised ground surrounded by a ditch comes into prominent view. Known locally as "the Harbour," it is thought to be the site of St. Anthony's chapel, which is mentioned in the 1538 survey of Wetheral priory. The name "Harbour" suggests that it was a place of safety. Monks from the priory are thought to have been buried there and it is reputed to be haunted.

During the early part of the 19th century cattle and pigs were allowed to roam around the village, feeding on the common and the roadsides. A "furthman," appointed annually, looked after them and saw that they did no damage in their search for food. So agile did some of these creatures become that one Wetheral farmer is said to have had pigs "as lish as grey hounds that could loup a six-barred yat."

At that time the village had its own carpenter, tailor, shoemaker, tanner, blacksmith and even a dancing master who taught a "Quadrilles class" in the Crown Hotel! The villagers made their own candles from mutton tallow and brewed very potent ale and wines, especially cowslip wine made from the cowslips which grew in such profusion thereabouts.

Fuel was mainly wood because there was no coal nearer than Hallbankgate. The only means of conveyance was by horse and cart and carriers made their living bringing coal to the village and lime for the fields for the farmers.

Whenever a farmer wanted to lime a field his neighbours would send their horses and carts to help him get the job done quickly and he, in turn, would do likewise for his neighbours. These communal jobs were always followed by enormous meals at which at lot of home brewed ale was drunk and merry evenings usually followed.

On one occasion a farmer whose land was being limed and who had the reputation of being "a gey near 'un" brought him lime leaders bread and cheese and ale at the end of the day instead of the expected generous meal. In those days this fare was usually served at a funeral, so the lime leaders took the farmer into a field, laid him in a furrow and set about covering him with soil. He soon got the message; and never again were his lime leaders deprived of their dinner and an evening's jollity.

Soon after they were landscaped, Corby Walks were thrown open to the general public by the Howard family annually on Easter Sunday; and so popular was this event, which came to be known as Corby Fair, that people were attracted to it from near and far. In the days before Wetheral viaduct was built a boat was used to row those from Wetheral across to Corby. On Easter Sunday, 1792, crossing took longer than usual because the Eden was in flood and the crowd waiting on the Wetheral bank were becoming impatient. Dick Gaddes, the strong, young oarsman could appreciate the annoyance at his delay but the river was high and he had the lives of the passengers to consider. On one trip so many people got into the boat it became overloaded to such an extent that only a small part of it remained above the swirling, swift-flowing water. Very carefully Dick Gaddes pulled away from the shore. The passengers threw anxious looks at the angry, brown flood water but remained seated and quiet because most knew Dick Gaddes to be a capable oarsman, very experienced and not one to take unnecessary risks. All went well until, in mid-stream, a stupid young man called Foster, thinking himself to be a clever-clogs stood up and began to rock the boat to frighten the women. Immediately panic ensued and people in the boat began to scream and shriek. Hearing the cries for help, people on both banks were eager to help but there was little they could do. They could see that the boat was sinking and shouted encouragement to Dick Gaddes who was pulling for the shore as hard as he could. The horrified spectators tore branches from the trees and attempted to wade out to help those in the boat; but with no success. The river was too deep and too fast. At length Dick Gaddes managed to get the boat within reach of the branches held out by the rescuers. One by one the passengers were landed, except for two men who were drowned and a little girl who floated downstream for about fifty yards before being pulled, exhausted, from the river. The two young men who were drowned were not local people. They were to have gone to London the following week to start their careers.

When angry the Eden is quite capable of wreaking considerable damage as John Mason discovered to his cost on Candlemas Day, 1822. He owned a cottage that stood on the bank of the river. On that fateful day the flood water rose higher than anyone could remember and, at first, the terrified tenants of the cottage remained inside it, hoping against hope that the water would stop rising.

When their neighbours realised their peril they came to the rescue and, with great difficulty, managed to get them out through the cottage's small windows. It was a painfully slow operation because the windows had not been built for large humans to pass through and, to make matters worse, the wife had to be carried out wrapped in a blanket and carrying her new-born child.

Within minutes of the family being pulled clear of their cottage home it collapsed and was washed away.

Yet despite its tragedies and near calamities, Wetheral has a happy history. It is a contented place, well pleased with itself, and with not a hint of melancholy clinging to its red sandstone buildings. Simply to wander around this beautiful village, absorbing its sheer perfection is bliss. The pleasant grouping of church, green, rectory, inns and fine houses makes it a never failing source of enchantment. And all around is the rolling agricultural landscape of the Eden Valley, guarded by Cold Fell and Cross Fell on the east and Penrith to the south-west. If you walk a lot there are tracks, quiet country roads, bridle paths and marked ways, all itching to be used. Unlike a lot of villages today, Wetheral is not dying on its feet. It is a healthy mix of families young and old and the groove in which these people live is a comfortable one.

*   *   *

From the riverside path out of Wetheral there is a last glimpse of the priory gatehouse and the field in front of it where the women of Wetheral used to sun-bleach their webs of spun linen. Then you are through a kissing gate and in the National Trust property of Wetheral Woods.

Sadly Dutch elm disease has devastated all the elms which once added such distinction to this lovely wood. All the stricken ones are now being felled and replaced with other kinds of tree, like oak, ash and beech. This work is well advanced. Meanwhile the extra sunlight now able to filter to the floor of the wood is proving to be of great benefit to a wide variety of plants providing ground cover, among them the ferns, campions, anemones, bluebells, primroses, celandines and lords and ladies. Many of the trees are hung with a variety of ivies, honeysuckles, vetches and travellers joy, all of which are responding favourably to the extra sunshine.

From the path as it begins to climb around the top of a cliff you get some fine views of an artificial island that had been built by the monks and the medieval fish traps.

The position is now about forty feet above the river, standing at the top of a rough flight of steps which has been cut into the sandstone cliffs, giving easy access to another of Wetheral's sources of interest, three chambers, each roughly 20 feet by 10 feet by 9 feet high. Each chamber, or cell, leads off a passage 3 feet wide and about 26 feet long. Windows in the outer wall allow daylight into these cells and the same wall has a fireplace and a chimney in the middle of it. These impressive cells, known as "The Caves" or "Wetheral Safeguards" or "St. Constantine's Cells," are thought to date from pre-Roman times. They are thought to have been associated with St. Constantine, the local patron saint, who was supposed to have been King of the Britons in the early days of Christianity and to have put aside the crown to become a missionary under St. Kentigern. However, Constantine was an enigmatic figure, sometimes referred to as a 6th century prince and at others as a 10th century king, so his link with Wetheral's caves is slender.

With the monks of the priory we are on much firmer ground. They most certainly used the caves for hiding their valuables, grain and dependents when the pillaging Scots carried out their swift and savage raids, burning, destroying and driving off the cattle.

In those days the only way into the cells was through a door at the end of the passage several feet above a narrow ledge that ran beneath it. Access was difficult, up a ladder which could be lowered and drawn up again. Overhanging shrubs and other vegetation rendered the entrance almost invisible.

Soft sandstone attracts graffiti as nectar attracts bees and there is much evidence of this in and around the cells. Several yards downstream of them and a few feet above the river are two Roman inscriptions, one of which is the equivalent of "Kilroy was here." Maximus scri(p)sit it reads, which translated from the Latin, says "Maximus wrote this" and refers to the XXth legion.

The earliest recorded inscription in the cells themselves reads T.Monte 1573 and many other people have carved their names in and around them since. But top marks for skill and originality must go to

Major William H.Mounsey of Rockcliffe, two of whose many carvings near the Eden are close to the cells. The first quotation, half-way down the steps and close to a symmetrical star of David reads:-

     Y   DDEILEN HON NEUS CYNDYFED GWYNT
     3   GWAE HI O'I THYNGED!
     I   HI HEN ELENI GANED!
           O MΛ 23AD 1852

It is a verse from the songs of Llywarch Hen, a Welsh poet of the early 9th century and means "This leaf which is being persecuted by the wind, let her beware of her fate: She is old though only born this year" M.W.H. Cut vertically are Mounsey's initials in reverse order. The symbol MΛ is Scorpio, the Scorpion, one of the signs of the Zodiac.

The second inscription is about twenty yards downstream from the first, a few feet above the river. It reads:-

     To meet the Atlantic's boundless time,
     See old Ituna's waters glide,
     As rolls the river to the sea
     So time unto eternity.
     O. M. Vo. A.D. 1852
     YESNUOM SUMLEILVG

Ituna is the Roman name for the River Eden. V is the sign of Aries, the Ram. The capital letters below the date spell GULIELMUS MOUNSEY written backwards. Gulielmus is the Latinised form of William.

Before leaving Wetheral Woods the way crosses a small bridge, goes down some steps and crosses a second bridge before passing close to a coast redwood, a member of the tallest growing tree species in the world. This is home to the pied flycatcher and the wood warbler. Some 200 yards upstream of this tall tree sees the upstream end of both Wetheral Woods and, across the river, the woods of Corby castle.

On leaving the wood we enter a clearing in which stands an important utility, Wetheral pumping station. Here the largest debris from the river water is removed before the water is pumped to Cumwhinton Water Works, there to have further treatment before it enters the mains supply for the whole Carlisle area.

The broad farm track winds its merry way up Primrose Bank and arrives at Cote House Farm, which sits astride the hilltop overlooking a steep, wooded bank. It is a farm with a difference, having been built in the late 16th century as a bastel-house. During the frequent Scottish raids of that period, cattle were concealed in the ground floor which was windowless. Upstairs the farmer, his family and farm workers would sit out the sieges which were usually short-lived, having got there up a removable ladder. A lot of bastel-houses and fortified pele towers were built in northern Cumbria between the 14th and 16th centuries.

Across a stile begins the descent to the river. At first the way is between confining trees. Then, suddenly, they are behind us and we find ourselves held enraptured by a vista of exquisite beauty. The hillside, richly garnished with deciduous greenery and speckled with flowers, falls away to a tree-lined meadow which spreads flatly to the Eden. This is pleasant enough but what catches and holds the eye is a place in the middle distance where the river changes course at the foot of a steep, tree-covered bank. There, in great swirls of foliage, this greenwood takes on an almost unreal quality. Sunlight dancing on the river increases the unreality. All is harmony and peace; and we could be looking not at the reality of the Eden but at the strange, enigmatic world that becomes alive in Tolkien's trilogy "The Lord of the Rings."

All is not what it seems. On closer inspection the meadow at the foot of the hill does not form part of the river's left bank but is firmly placed in mid-stream. It is an island that had been reclaimed as part of the dig-for-victory effort during World War II. Mallards build their nests on the edge of this hayfield, which is also home to grey wagtails, dippers and moorhens. You may see a kingfisher if you are very lucky; but if it sees you first, you won't.

A path, which keeps close to the river bank, takes us past exotic Himalayan balsam and wild tansy to a stile leading to a small wood.

Cote House Tower Farm, on the right approaching the wood, was built in the 1840s. The tall tower rising; from the middle of it was used as an observation post from where watch could be kept for salmon poachers. Some of today's salmon poachers cannot be seen from this tower because they are so small. They live locally, are savage killers and are called mink.

A little way into the wood a large tombstone has been positioned alongside the path. Despite tall tales of rough justice administered to those caught poaching salmon, it has no fishy connections. Nevertheless there is an interesting tale attached to it. At one time there were three "freestone" quarries along the river in Wetheral parish where local parishioners could take what stones they required, paying only the wages of the quarryman and the mason, the stone itself being free. In the early part of the 19th century a local quarryman, Matthew Knublay, made this headstone for his parents. But they were buried in a different parish so Matthew decided to erect the stone where it is today because he was not allowed to remove it from the parish from where it had been freely obtained.

For several wonderful miles our way travels upstream, now crossing pastures, now following woodland tracks, mostly only a few feet above the level of the water but now and again, where cliffs tower thin tracks crawl along narrow ledges which rise high above the water. It is a walk into a world of quiet timelessness, flavoured with the excitement of healthy adventure.

An island - and there are several - is a boon to the one whose land edges the river because it enables him to fish from four banks instead of two while the salmon are squeezed into two narrow channels until the island is passed.

5: Armathwaite to Kirkoswald

Length of section: 5 miles
Total distance: 30 miles
Map: O.S.Landranger 86
Handy hostelries: Fetherston Arms Hotel,
     The Crown Inn, The Black Bull.

Route Directions

From the Fox and Pheasant take the pleasant lane that goes parallel to the river but separated from it by a field. This is the only public right of way into Coombs Wood; the riverside path being private. A broad ride leads very pleasantly through Coombs Wood to where a gate in a wall leads to a road. All other paths in Coombs Wood are private.

Turn right, along this road, which edges the wood to its end then curves away to the left, downhill, to pass Beck Farm. It then climbs steadily passing two side roads joining from the left to mile-and-a-bit distant Nunnery Walks, clearly signed.

Turn in to the hotel grounds at the Nunnery. A small payment is required to explore Nunnery Walks, which are very worthwhile. At the meeting of Croglin Beck and the Eden take a downstream path, which covers a sizeable piece of the river missed by the road walking.

On leaving the Nunnery, turn right and continue along the road, crossing Croglin Beck and passing Staffield Hall on your right. At the far end of the building enter a field on your right through a gate and go along an ill-defined right of way, first keeping close to a boundary wall on your right then, keeping in the same direction, cross a large field along the side of ground that rises on your left to where the way becomes well defined and leads to the outskirts of Kirkoswald. When the tarmac road is reached take it, deeper into the village, down its steep street and into the little square with its three welcoming pubs, the end of the section.

Armathwaite to Kirkoswald

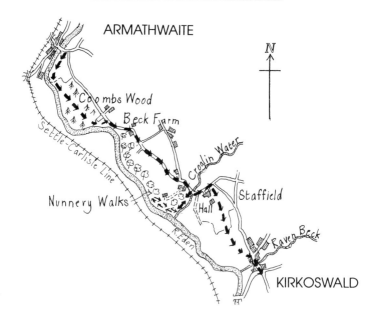

The Background Story

The Red Lion, Armathwaite, was up for sale. The notice read:-

> To be sold by Auction upon the Premises on Thursday evening, February 10th, 1803, all that Freehold Messuage and Tenement known by the sign of the Red Lion situate on Armathwaite Bridge, on the banks of the Eden.
>
> As a private residence the Red Lion Inn (from the beautiful scenery around it) is particularly adapted for the reception of a genteel family. Here indeed the complete sportsman may properly be said to be in his own element having a most prolific salmon and trout stream at hand and, at a trifling distance, plenty of heath where grouse and other game may be found in abundance.
>
> There are also several families of distinction in the neighbourhood where a gentleman of character and connections will meet with comfortable society.

Several families of distinction still live in and around the beautiful village of Armathwaite, "the clearing of the hermit," which nestles so snugly in an arboreal hollow beside the Eden. Many visitors are attracted to it in search of peace, serenity and magnificent riverside walking. Others go there because of the fine salmon fishing. The Red Lion is now the Fox and Pheasant.

Armathwaite has another pub, The Duke's head, which, like the Fox and Pheasant is well patronised by anglers because fishing is a thirsty job. There is a post office-cum-shop in the village, a food store, a hall which was built by Armathwaite Women's Institute and a lovely little chapel which was built in the middle of the seventeen century. At one time the chapel was in a very dilapidated condition and used as a cattle shed. But today this chapel, now the church of Christ and Mary, is a credit to Armathwaite's caring folk. It sits on an eminence near the castle.

Armathwaite castle is sited on a rock washed by the Eden. It occupies the site of an ancient fortress and commands wonderful views of the river which thereabouts is flanked with lovely, wooded banks and sandstone outcrops.

The family of Skelton of Armathwaite castle was one of great antiquity with roots in Skelton village, near Penrith. It represented the area of Carlisle in parliament between the reigns of Edward II and Henry VIII and distinguished itself in both French and Scottish wars. In the first year of the reign of Edward IV John Skelton received a grant from the Crown of 100 acres of forest at a place called Armathwaite Bank. Whether or not this was before the Skeltons took possession of the Armathwaite Castle Estate is not certain for the two estates are mentioned separately in a judicial enquiry taken in the reign of Henry VIII. It is, however, a matter of historical fact that the Skeltons owned both castle and forest as a combined estate until 1712 when it was sold to William Sanderson Esq. On the death of Robert Sanderson Milbourne in 1822 the manor was held by trustees until 1846 when it was purchased by the 2nd Earl of Lonsdale. Both Castle estate and manor were sold by the 5th Earl to Edward Ecroyd of Low House in 1888. The castle was sold to a firm of builders in 1946 and has now been converted into flats.

A sword bearing the inscription "Edwardvs - Prins Anglic" in gold on its blade used to hang in the castle. It was probably left there in the time of Edward I whose son is thought to have lodged at Armathwaite while his father was at Lannercost. The sword was probably removed from the castle when the Skeltons sold the property.

The Settle-Carlisle line passes close above the village but the station has been closed. However, periodically Dales Rail trains stop there because Armathwaite, a lovely village in its own right, makes an ideal base from which to explore the Lower Eden Valley.

A bridge was built across the Eden at Armathwaite in 1700 to replace two fords over which went what was once the main road to Newcastle. The bridge lasted for just over two centuries until 1908 when it was replaced by the present one.

Cross the bridge from west to east, follow the quiet, meandering, uphill road signposted Ainstable and in a little over a mile you will be in that tiny village which, being quiet, attractive and full of tradition and heritage is typical of so many Eden Valley villages.

East of Ainstable, in Broomriggs plantation, are the ancient stone circles of Broomriggs and Grey Yauds, tucked away in the resin-scented darkness of the fir trees. A good mile north-east of this wood and hugging the sides of Cumrew, Newbiggin and Croglin Fells is the village of Newbiggin, which means "new building" and shares its name with at least nine other Cumbrian villages.

From Newbiggin with its panoramic views across the surrounding countryside with Saddleback silhouetted on the skyline in the south-west, there is an excellent walk along a bridleway north-eastwards into the Pennines to what was once the King's Forest of Geltsdale, a hunting preserve. Little of the original forest remains and much of the walk is through open moorland along a horseshoe-shaped course which drops down to either the village of Talkin or Castle Carrock.

* * *

Half a mile upstream from Armathwaite Bridge the river bends to the north-east, over the remains of a weir and frees itself from the Eden Gorge. This is a truly magnificent stretch of water, some three miles long. Aeons ago, when the river was young, it cut a twisting course through the red sandstone. Slowly, down the ages, as the sedimentary bedrock was worn away, so this majestic gorge developed. Today, much of it on both sides of the river is well wooded, the considerably expanse of Coombs Wood spreading upwards and away from the eastern bank for all of two miles and Baron Wood, almost as vast, covering a similar area on the west bank. Spaced at irregular intervals along both sides of the ravine sheer sandstone cliffs soar to great, tree-capped heights. Here Nature has created an awe-inspiring spectacle, a wonderland with the river running wide and, in parts, deep, now below tall cliffs, now between tangles of overhanging leafiness and, especially on the western side, clear areas.

Within the gorge and carved into one of the cliffs, which rises sheer from the water, is a phenomenon which few people, either visitors or Armathwaite residents, have ever seen. It takes the form of several quite large, round, ghost-like faces which are shown in relief on the rock face, close to a salmon shown in outline and several lines of poetry taken from Walton's *Compleat Angler*.

Clearly the artist or artists took time, for the faces have been very carefully sculpted and the letters of the poem are all well formed and clean cut. They read:-

> "Oh the fisher's gentle life
> Happiest is of any.
> Void of pleasure, full of strife
> And beloved by many.

Words by Isaac Newton in Compleat Angler, *carved by William Mounsey on the cliff face in the Eden gorge near Armathwaite. The third line is typical of Mounsey's humour. It should read ;*
Full of pleasure void of strife,
Note letter 's' carved in reverse - again typical Mounsey

> Other joys are but toys
> And to be lamented.
> Only this a pleasure is.
> Timber) (Fishing.

Next follows a line containing some Greek.

> Apiotos UEV UDWP

and finally

> Eden I.B. 1855.

William Mounsey had a hand in this, probably assisted by other members of his family. All the clues point in his direction, certainly as far as the poem is concerned. The third line has been turned back to front in typical Mounsey manner. It should read "FULL of pleasure VOID of strife." The carving has been worked deliberately in an Old English style with some of the letters back to front and old spelling.

It is thought that the poem was cut by several members of the Mounsey family, including William, while on a fishing expedition.

The faces, however, are of a different quality. Although they are found within close proximity of the poem and are beautifully made, they do not appear to carry the Mounsey stamp. Mr Peter Ecroyd, who owns that part of the river near the faces, believes they could be a great deal older than the writing. He has in his possession a Stuart fireplace over-mantel on which the same enigmatic faces are carved.

Further up the river, on a stretch owned by Lazonby Hall, are more carvings and the famous chain rock and cave which was once used by nuns as a hiding place from marauding Scots.

The Eden Gorge is wide. On a previous visit and with permission from the landowner, a friend and I had explored the other bank, looking for the faces in the rock from across the water. It had been a fascinating experience involving a lot of river level waking sometimes on a defined path, sometimes not, and the scaling of the side of a cliff that rose sheer from the river in which it had its feet. On one side of it we had made use of a rope "banister" placed there for the benefit of salmon fishers: on the other, had pulled ourselves up using the slim boles of young trees. The river when viewed from the greenery capping this huge outcrop had looked positively primeval. Now, from the other shore we could see clearly how the crag fitted into its surroundings and were suitably impressed. It's awful loftiness was breathtaking.

The otter, like the fox, the badger and the hare has been a part of the Eden Valley for thousands of years. Few, if any mammals have been around longer. It was resident in Britain before melting ice-water caused the formation of the North Sea which separated Britain from mainland Europe; and it is for this reason there is no distinct British species in its own right. British otters are members of the European otter family, *Lutra Lutra,* which extends throughout most of Europe and eastwards across northern Asia to Japan.

The otter is a member of the weasel family, the muskelids, and shares similar characteristics with many, but not all, of the other members of the group. It is an active hunter, has a long, sinuous body and comparatively short legs just like its cousins the ferret, mink, stoat, and weasel.

Although the otter is a mammal which makes its home on land it has adapted very well to life in a largely aquatic environment; and because its habitat and food supply are relatively specialised, it has become an increasingly vulnerable species. Ideally it needs a territory of several miles of undisturbed waterway with plenty of undergrowth and a plentiful supply of fish and eels, which make up the bulk of its diet.

Thankfully, for much of its length the Eden can still provide the kind of habitat so necessary for the otter's well-being. Though now much depleted in numbers it still makes use of this natural cover, although these days it is rarely seen.

Otters are now protected by law and serious attempts are being made to conserve the remaining otter population. Local riverside landowners hope that the Eden Gorge will become an otter sanctuary and that this once harassed creature will again thrive in its Eden Valley home.

* * *

It is a good mile, no more, and an enjoyable one at that from Coombs Wood to Nunnery Walks, one of the most beautiful riverside walks in all England. The road dips into a hollow to pass Beck Farm and takes its time climbing out again. The Benedictine convent, which gave the name "Nunnery" to its site close to the confluence of Croglin Beck and the Eden, had its beginnings in Carlisle when St. Cuthbert laid the first foundation there and gave the veil to Ermenburga, queen dowager of Northumberland, as first abbess. In 1089, William Rufus, the second Norman monarch, had it removed from the city to Armathwaite then called Heremitethwaite, where it remained for "some ages" before being re-established where the 18th century Nunnery House stands today. Rufus gave the community two acres of land on which to build the convent, two acres of meadow adjoining, a further three carucates (1) of land close to it and yet another 216 acres, including part of the Royal Forest of Inglewood, slightly further away. The nuns and their tenants had common pasturage and the right of free timber from the royal forest. The convent was dedicated to Our Saviour and the Blessed Virgin Mary.

---

(1) A carucate is a Norman measure of land, varying with the nature of the soil, being as much as could be tilled with one plough (8 oxen) in a year.

Whenever a vacancy occurred for the office of prioress, the nuns elected the person of their choice and then presented her to the bishop for appointing and induction.

Despite its land and privileges, the convent, never very affluent, was frequently poverty stricken. During the reign of Edward II, the King, having been made aware of the convent's poverty, sent ten pounds to the prioress to enable her to clear a debt for victuals incurred at Carlisle, since the nuns were not able to pay off so large an amount. The same King also waived their annual rent of £10 in consideration of the losses they had sustained during the Border Wars.

Because of its situation the convent suffered frequently from raiding Scots. In one raid, during the reign of Edward IV, it was almost destroyed and the Scots carried off jewels, relics, books, evidences and other property.

This sacking was followed by a Charter of Confirmation from the King of England and Ainstable church was appropriated to the convent. It was a time of new beginning and from then onwards the convent continued to flourish until about 1536 when it was surrendered to the commissioners of Henry VIII. At that time the community consisted of a prioress and three nuns.

The crown held the convent until the reign of Edward VI who, on March 9th, 1552, granted to "William Greyme, gentleman, the house and site of the late priory of Armathwaite." The Grahams owned the property until 1685 when George Graham Esq., sold it to Sir John Lowther, Bart., who swapped it with John Aglionby Esq., for Drumburgh Castle in 1694. John Aglionby took up residence there and his grandson, Henry, pulled down the old house, which formed part of the priory, and erected the pleasant mansion known today as Nunnery House. Part of the wall of the monastic building is still standing on the west side of the house.

To the north-east of the mansion, in a field called Cross Close, there is an upright pillar, the principal remaining part of the priory. On one side of it there is a large, oval stone with a cross in its centre, around which is inscribed "SANCTUARIUM 1088," which points to the convent holding the ancient privilege of sanctuary in common with many other religious houses in those times.

To the east of the mansion there is a small, square piece of land surrounded by tall trees. This used to be the priory's burial ground. Several interesting remains have been discovered there including the cowled head of a monk. This prompts the question: how did a monk come to be buried in the burial ground of a nunnery?

A little beyond this place is a well, Chapel Well.

The nunnery is now a hotel (teas etc. available) but nowadays is best known for its glorious walks, created by Henry Aglionby about 1750. They are circular and all begin at the car park outside Nunnery House (small fee payable) and pass through a small wood and across a field to where a map board indicates the short and longer walks and the hidden dangers of the lower paths. All the routes are very popular and all offer fine views of the Eden. The one past the summer-house, with its display of heraldic shields, is particularly pleasing because the superb views of the river are ever-present as the path drops almost to river level. The cliffs on the opposite bank are used by rock climbers and it is there that Sampson's Caves are sited. The path continues downriver as far as the fence at the end of the wood where it doubles back on itself a little closer to the waters' edge and goes back upstream to where Croglin Beck flows into it. On its outward journey the path, in descending to river level, crosses the top of a cliff. Much of its lower level return route is along spectacular, overhanging ledges that have been hewn from the cliff face. This makes for very exciting walking indeed at any time. With the Eden in angry spate the prospect is terrifying.

Of all the Eden's feeders, none can surpass Croglin Beck, where dippers build their nests beneath damp, rocky ledges, red squirrels forage among the leafy branches of tall trees and salmon in season, leap in the lower pools. It is a mountain stream in a hurry rushing at and leaping mossy ledges in its haste to join the Eden.

Rev. W.Ford, in his *Guide to the Lakes*, had this to say about Croglin Beck:

> "It may, we think, be safely asserted that the Croglin in this last part of its course for the space of a mile, during which it pours along a deep ravine, has no equal. It first enters this savage dell by a fall of forty feet, forcing its way into a deep caldron scooped out of the rock, in which the water is agitated and whirled around in boiling eddies till it finds an escape by a narrow opening in one corner, whence it rushes down several leaps,

foaming over the large masses that hinder its impetuous progress. The rocks are piled on each other up to the height of one or two hundred feet, projecting their bold fronts forward over the river, here scored with lightning, there with ivy green or grey with aged lichens and mosses."

Rev. Ford was spot on with his observations. Truly, this is a walk not to be missed.

The scattered village of Staffield spreads along the opposite side of the Croglin from the Nunnery. It is a fee of nearby Kirkoswald and took its name from a local family. When, during the reign of Henry V the co-heiresses married into the Carlisle families of Chambers, Mulcaster and Blennerhasset, the name became extinct. It subsequently became the property of the Fletchers of Hutton and the Lowthians, the last of whom, Richard Lowthian Ross, sold it to the Aglionbys of Nunnery. The village common was enclosed, Mr Ross bought land adjoining the Croglin and planted several thousand trees on its eastern bank, which much improved the Nunnery's scenery.

A public footpath, undefined for much of the way, leads nicely from the corner of Staffield Hall to Kirkoswald and from it the well-cared for rolling countryside is seen to advantage.

For many years Kirkoswald has been the winner of Cumbria's best kept village competition. Many of its houses are early 18th century and as neat as new pins, the red sandstone of its buildings is pleasing to the eye and its hillside situation is admirable. So when electricity and telephone lines began to criss-cross the street like a spider's web, the proud inhabitants persuaded the authorities to re-route them underground at a cost of £12,000 and the environment is the better for it.

Two pubs face each other across the tiny village square, The Crown Inn and The Black Bull. A third, a 19th century coaching house, now a family hotel, The Fetherston Arms Hotel, stands just across the street from the square. All are well worth visiting.

Kirkoswald Church

6:   Kirkoswald to Langwathby

Length of section: 6 miles
Total distance: 36 miles
Map: O.S. Landranger 86 and 91
Handy hostelries: The Shepherds Inn.

Route Directions

From Kirkoswald take the Lazonby road as far as the Eden bridge where, immediately before it, take the signposted way upstream. At first this keeps away from the river. Once in the first pasture go left, keeping close to the hedge on your left to a field gate which go through and then right, keeping close to the hedge on your right and continue until the river is reached. Turn left along the river bank and keep close to it until a country road is reached on your left. Join the road briefly to cross a stream before going along a clearly defined path at the end of a lay-by on your right, through a wood. Leave the shallow wood up some steps and over a stile in a pasture. Go diagonally to the right to rejoin the river and continue along its bank first across a field's edge then, following markers, through a long riverside wood, passing, en route, the Lacy Caves. Once past them the path becomes broader and soon a viaduct carrying the Settle-Carlisle line over the Eden is seen on your right.

Where a narrower path leads off, parallel at first to the one you are on, and separated from it by a fence on your right, take it to where it crosses some old sidings and passes a building on its right to join a tarmac road at the entrance to land belonging to Long Meg Mines. Follow the tarmac road first uphill then levelling out alongside the Settle-Carlisle line on your right, beyond which there are fine views of the meandering river. Go all the way to Little Salkeld where turn left, uphill, to enter the village.

At the tiny village green take the right-hand road downhill, past The Watermill near its foot and, because the land adjacent to the river is private, keep along it until Langwathby, where the end of the section is reached.

Kirkoswald to Langwathby

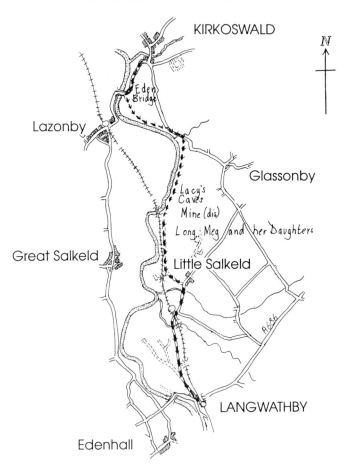

The Background Story

Towards the end of the 16th century the Fetherstonhaugh family took up residence in Kirkoswald and their offspring built the Fetherston Arms in local red sandstone as a coaching inn. It lost its pub licence in 1947 and became a fishing hotel with its own water until 1975 when a private syndicate took over the fishing. It regained its pub licence in 1985 and ever since has been run as a free house with a well deserved reputation.

The village has a castle with a tunnel leading to the nearby church of St. Oswald, it is said. Randolph Engayn built it *circa* 1200 and it was subsequently enlarged and greatly improved by the addition of a park which was enclosed by Sir Huge de Morville to whom it had come, along with the manor of Kirkoswald and Lazonby with his wife, Helwise de Stuteville. And what a splendid castle it was! The great hall was ornamented with portraits of the kings of England from "Brute" downwards and for a considerable period had the reputation of being one of the finest halls in the north of England. The Morville family held the castle until it came into the hands of the Multons when it received considerable additions from Thomas de Multon and John de Castro. About the beginning of the 16th century its defences were further strengthened by the construction of a ditch. From the Multon's, the castle with the manor of Kirkoswald and Lazonby, descended to the Dacres. It was on the orders of Lord Dacre of the south that it was dismantled. In 1688 the castle was "little more than a bare shell on a heap of stones."

Tradition has it that a subterranean passage connects the castle with the parish church and this is partly corroborated by the fact that a stream which runs under the church became thick and muddy when the castle moat was cleaned out.

The church stands at the south end of Kirkoswald, a quarter of a mile west of the castle, mid-way between it and the Eden and on much lower ground. All of it except its bell-tower was built in 1897 to replace a wooden one.

The first Christian church on the site was consecrated by St. Aiden in the 7th century when he and Oswald, King of Northumbria, came across people worshipping a spring and converted them to Christianity. The church was built over a stream of pure water flowing from this spring, which is at the eastern side of the building.

All that remains of the castle at Kirkoswald

A flight of steps at the west end of the church leads down to the water which, judging by the sample I sipped, has not deteriorated with age.

The church is a neat, almost square structure with Norman and pointed arches supported on three large pillars which separate the aisle from the nave. St. Peter and St. Paul are depicted in beautifully stained glass, as are the coats of arms of some prominent local families including the Dacres, the Fetherstonhaughs, the Howards and the Musgraves.

Some fine old lime trees line both sides of the path that winds through the churchyard and overarch it, a leafy, green canopy in summer, a delicate tangle of bare branches in winter, a delight all the year round.

During the first decade of the 14th century a pele tower was built at the bottom of the hill in Kirkoswald to help protect the village from Scottish raiders. Unfortunately it did not come up to expectations and in 1314 the Scots attacked the village and set fire to it.

In 1597 forty-two Kirkoswald folk fell victim to the plague, which struck again the following year when a staggering 583 people caught it.

Tuesday is market day and the charter by which it is held was granted to Huge de Morville by King John while he was in Kirkoswald on February 25th, 1201.

Kirkoswald, built along the banks of Raven Beck, is amply supplied with water, which accounts for the paper mill, the saw and bobbin mill, the mill for carding and spinning wool, the corn mill and the brewery, which once flourished there. However agriculture was and remains the main source of employment within Kirkoswald parish.

The soil in the western part is very rich and productive. In other parts the soil is heavy with a clayey subsoil, whilst in yet others it is light with a sandy subsoil. All this favours arable farming and the parish of Kirkoswald is very productive in all kinds of farm produce.

A short distance from Kirkoswald the Eden is crossed by a bridge of two large and two small arches. It was built in 1762 and links Kirkoswald to Lazonby, "the freedman's settlement." A little upstream of this beautiful 18th century structure is another that is a product of the 20th century, Lazonby's very fine, open air, heated swimming pool. It was built in 1964, thanks to the efforts of local people who brought a dream to reality and joy to their children.

Bridge over the Eden between Lazonby and Kirkoswald

Beyond the pool and set back from the Eden is the village of Lazonby itself, built, for the most part, on both sides of one long sloping street. Its church is dedicated to St. Nicholas, patron saint of children, many of whose local fathers are dedicated to "The Midland Hotel," Lazonby's neat pub, which is built close to and down from Lazonby railway station on the Settle-Carlisle line. Immediately on leaving Lazonby, heading south, the Settle-Carlisle line leaps across the village on a fine red sandstone bridge.

Lazonby station was once very busy. Passenger traffic was good and the goods traffic lively. Movement of cattle and sheep was heavy, especially during the autumnal sheep sales when as many as sixty wagon loads were moved on the big sale days.

Lazonby advertises itself as "the foremost greyfaced lamb centre," and when you consider that during the back end sales upwards of 16,000 lambs can change hands for between £750,000 and a million pounds at one sale, that is no idle boast. A greyfaced lamb or a mule is a cross between the Swaledale ewe and the blue-faced Leicester tup. It is a good-bodied sheep with a speckled head and feet and a curly fleece. Breeders throughout the land are interested in it for crossing with the Suffolk tup for mutton production.

Fifty years ago greyfaced lambs were to be found only on the fells within a fifteen mile radius of Alston. Today, tens of thousands are sold at Lazonby mart every year. But these days it is cattle wagons of the road, not the rail variety that are usually used for transporting the lambs to their various destinations.

* * *

The path from Lazonby bridge follows the eastern bank of the Eden for a pleasant mile to join a country road for just long enough to cross a beck. Then it returns to the quiet of the river to become even more pleasant clinging close to the foot of a hill along the riverbank. At first crossing open pasture it enters a long wood where, rising and falling with the lie of the land, it snakes along in a most exciting way. Sometimes reeds, tall grasses and tangles of thin branches encroach. At others it winds between tall trees and at one point, close to river level, it runs straight between the trunks of young trees too evenly spaced not to have been planted by man. Where the path climbs across the edge of a sandstone cliff an insignificant-looking trod dips steeply down towards the river far below and vanishes. It leads to the Lacy Caves, the main entrance of which is clearly seen once the brow of the cliff has been crossed and the path has lost height.

The caves, five large chambers linked by arched entrances, are dark despite windows overlooking the river which laps at the base of the cliff some distance below. Between the windows and the river there is a narrow ledge and it is to this ledge that the narrow trod dips so steeply from the path close to the cliff's brow. Lt. Col. Samuel Lacy had the caves built in the 18th century so that his Salkeld Hall estate would have a feature in-keeping with the romantic taste of the time and to ensure that his surname would be perpetuated.

The way, broad and clear now, continues up the steep, heavily wooded hill, high above the river that bends around it, tumbling and roaring over the remains of a stony mill-dam.

Upstream of this old mill, where the river flows unruffled, the Settle-Carlisle line crosses it diagonally on a fine viaduct, touching the eastern bank close to Long Meg, from where anhydrate and gypsum are mined.

From Long Meg the way becomes a tarmac road from where panoramic views are obtained of the river and its environs; and at the end of this road lies Little Salkeld.

The watermill at Little Salkeld is one of the few remaining country corn mills still producing stoneground flours the traditional way by waterpower. For almost fifteen years Nick Jones and his wife have been using the mill to produce flour from organically-grown grain. They employ a full-time miller and three part-time staff to make ten different flours and produce about four tonnes a week.

Most flours contain a high proportion of imported wheat whereas British wheat, which The Watermill uses, produces a tastier if slightly denser bread and the milling process is simple and traditional. The wheat is dried slowly, cleaned and then milled through slowly turning granite burr stones. Nothing is added, nothing is taken away. Milling through cool running millstones ensures that even distribution of the wheatgerm whose oils give the flour much of its flavour and nutritional value. Modern high-speed milling using rollers involves separating out the bran and the wheatgerm and the heat generated can reduce the nutritional value of the grain. Most wholemeal flours are milled from non-organic wheat and any spray residues tend to accumulate on the outer bran layer. By using grain grown to organic principles The Watermill ensures than any chemical spray or fertilizer residue in the flour is minimal.

The land on which the grain used at The Watermill is grown is farmed in a way that allows sustained fertility and an ecologically sound system of husbandry. The use of clean, self-renewing and energy efficient water-power at The Watermill ensures than minimal demands are made on earth's finite energy reserves.

At the 1987 Royal Show at Stoneleigh, Warwickshire, Nick Jones won the prestigious Food From Britain Award for his new organic flour, a blend which included wheat, barley, rye and oats. Not bad for a small Eden milling firm which works to the simple axiom:

> Before the flour the mill.
> Before the mill, the grain,
> Before the grain.
> The sun, the earth, the rain.

Once a bridge spanned the Eden between Little Salkeld and much

Great Salkeld Church with fortified tower

larger Great Salkeld on its west bank but it was washed away in a flood in 1360 and a replacement was never built.

Second only to Stonehenge in size, the mysterious stone circle known as Long Meg and her Daughters stands a short distance away from and to the north of Little Salkeld.

When William Wordsworth visited the site in 1833, Long Meg and her Daughters maintained an enigmatic silence and he found this irritating.

> "Speak Thou, whose massy strength and stature scorn
> The power of years - pre-eminent, and placed
> Apart, to overlook the circle vast -
> Speak, Giant Mother"

This flattering request from Lakeland's exalted poet deserved an answer. Yet Long Meg told him nothing, which was a pity for she had much to tell.

There are more than 900 Megalithic rings in Great Britain and Long Meg and her Daughters, though not one of the earliest, is one of the largest and finest. The name comes from a legend that an angry saint turned a local coven of witches into stone. Another myth claims that the granite stones of the circle were Long Meg's lovers. Long Meg herself, the circle's outlier, is a 3.7m tall block of new red sandstone. Her surfaces are smooth and tabular and on the face nearest the circle there are three markings, a cup and ring with gutter, a spiral and some incomplete concentric circles. The signs are enigmatic and may not be contemporary with the erection of the stones.

Tradition states that if a piece is broken off Long Meg, the stone will bleed, but perhaps Long Meg's association with "the wondrous wizard" of Kelso, Michael Scott, is the strangest of all. Scott, who was born in 1175 and died in 1230 and who practised astrology in Palermo, somehow managed to advance through the time barrier and returned to a 17th century England where, having "cleft the Eildon Hills in twain," he endowed Long Meg's stones with magical power so that no one could count them twice and get the same answer!

The site is a big one, the huge stones being set out in a flattened circle, 109.4m x 93.0m. The largest of the seventy-odd granite stones weighs about 28 tons and would have required at least 120 people to erect it. The average weight of the stones is ten tons; and it has been calculated (R.J.C.Atkinson in 1961 and J.M.Coles in 1973) that some sixty people would have been required to drag each of the stones up the sloping site and haul it upright.

If only one 10 hour day was needed to find a suitable stone, lever it onto rollers or a sled, lash it securely and drag it as much as half a mile uphill to the site, dig a hole for it to stand in, erect the stone in it and jam it tightly with packing stones, the construction of Long Meg and her Daughters would have taken 42,000 man hours plus the time taken to build the 3.6m wide bank around the circle's circumference.

Long Meg and her Daughters, being a stone circle within a bank is a stone henge. Some six miles to the south-west, near Penrith, there is an associated henge called King Arthur's Round Table; a circular earthen enclosure with a bank and an inner ditch; and the fact that the two circles are so close together gives some indication of the density of the local Neolithic population.

It was once thought that Long Meg contained two burial chambers. In 1586 William Camden reported that inside the ring were "two heaps of stones, under which they say are dead bodies bury'd."

However, a footnote in the 1695 edition of *Britannia* said that the heaps "are no part of it; have been thrown up here in a waste corner of the field" (Camden 1695:831). The cairns have long since vanished and, in any case, were not prehistoric.

Long Meg is within three day's walk of the Langdale Stone axe factory. Stone axes were used extensively in the construction of Long Meg and other stone circles. Rough cut outs of these axes were carried from the factories along mountain tracks to be ground and polished at sites where suitable sandstone was available.

Standing on the route towards the Tyne Gap, Long Meg is one of eight circle henges along the 350 miles between Fife and Wiltshire which share similar characteristics. Each has a large open ring within a smallish henge and each is on a trackway in an area of Neolithic occupation. Some 2,000 Neolithic people are thought to have occupied the areas immediately around the Lake District mountains, living in the 200 square miles of cultivated land there. Between 400 and 500 of them were involved in ceremonies at Long Meg.

Often in the larger megalithic rings the compass points - north, south, east and west - are marked by larger stones. At Long Meg only due east and west are marked in this way. To the Neolithic arable farmers and stockbreeders looking for signs of the return of warmer weather this was very important for at the spring and autumn equinoxes, half-way between its summer and winter solstices, the sun rises in the east and sets in the west.

Long Meg herself, the outlier at the south-west of the circle, stands in the right place to relate to a midwinter sunset but only if seen from the middle of a ring with a flattened arc, making its centre difficult to determine. Yet such was the skill of the ring's builders that Long Meg is aligned so that the midwinter sun would have set exactly over it. For this to happen its top would have had to rise clear of the skyline, hence Long Meg's height.

Of the seventy known stone circles with outliers spread down the western side of Britain whose azimuths have been properly recorded, there were no constant orientations. So it is thought that in some cases an outlier's function would be as a signpost for travellers to and from the site. Long Meg stands close to the crest of a ridge beyond which the ground falls away steeply to the Eden on its west side. Anyone approaching from that direction can see the top of Long Meg outlined against the sky from as far as a mile away when all the other stones are hidden by the curve of the hill. Perhaps Long Meg had a dual function.

The entrance to Long Meg's circle is in the same position as the outlier and could be associated with the midwinter sunset. The gaps in the henge banks are merely secondary entrances and have no astronomical connotations. Similarly there is no evidence that the people who built Long Meg used its once impressive principal entrance other than as a means of access to the circle.

The Eden at Bolton Bridge

7: Langwathby to Appleby

Length of section:	15 miles
Total distance:	51 miles
Map:	O.S. Landranger 90 and 91
Handy hostelries:	King's Head, Tufton Arms,
	Crown and Cushion.
	There are several cafés in the town.

Route Directions

From Langwathby to Culgaith the way is along the B6412 which keeps fairly close to the Eden's eastern bank throughout. Although for some 3.5 miles the walking is on tarmac or a grassy verge, there are many fine views of the Eden from this elevated vantage point. At Culgaith keep to the B6412 as it bends sharply to the left but where it bends sharply to the right at the end of the village, continue straight ahead either over a stile and up a field, keeping close to a wall on your right to enter another field at the far end of it, or use the lane to the right of the wall to reach the same spot. Go diagonally left across this second field to a point in the wall on the far side of it, some three-quarters of the way along it, to enter another field over a stile close to its left-hand boundary wall. Keeping close to the wall on your left, go to the far end of this field and continue, crossing another stile next to a gate along a well defined track, downhill, through woods to a tarmac road. Go downhill along it to the village of Newbiggin. On approaching the village cross Crowdundle Beck along the tarmac road then immediately turn right, following the direction of the signpost downstream, over a stile, through a field, under a viaduct carrying the Settle-Carlisle line and cross another field, ignoring the bridge over the beck, to enter the wooded grounds of Acorn Bank over another stile.

Take the beckside path, first along the stream's bank, then up a short, steep slope to the rear of Acorn Bank and, keeping close to the lovely old building on your left, go to the large gates at the corner of this manor house. There, close to these gates, go through a much smaller one into a field which, on the side of it fronting Acorn Bank,

Langwathby to Appleby

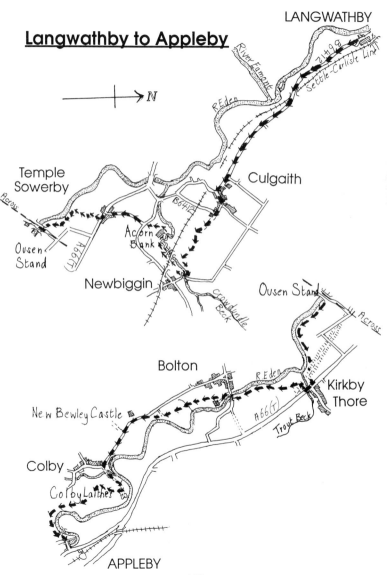

LANGWATHBY

River Eamont

R.Eden

Settle-Carlisle Line

A 6 8 6

→N

Temple
Sowerby

Across

Ousen
Stand

A66(T)

B6412

Acorn
Bank

Culgaith

Newbiggin

Crowdundle
Beck

Ousen Stand

Across

Bolton

R.Eden

New Bewley Castle

A66(T)

Kirkby
Thore

Trout Beck

Colby

Colby Laithes

APPLEBY

instead of a fence there is a ha-ha.

Cross the field diagonally, aiming for a T junction which can be seen beyond the field's far hedge. There is a pronounced dip in the middle of this field which is at first unseen when you begin the crossing. A wide drainage ditch flows along the bottom of it but this is crossed by a bridge with a stile. So the way ahead to the T junction is clearly defined.

Go straight ahead along the upright of the T, a pleasant, quiet road which will bring you into Temple Sowerby. Once there, use the road between the church on your left and the pub on your right to the A66 on its way through the village, which cross and walk towards the eastern end of the place. Where a signposted tarmac road leads off to the right, go along it, up a small hill, and continue straight ahead along an unsurfaced lane. Soon a gate into a field marks what appears to be the lane end; but the lane makes a right-angled left-hand turn and continues on its way. Go along it to a stile on your right, which cross and continue, first on the level, then steeply down a hillside to the river seen ahead.

On reaching the Eden, turn left and go upstream between the abutment of a demolished railway bridge and the river and climb to the top of a wooden bank immediately beyond it. Continue along the top of the bank, close to the trees on your right, passing Temple Sowerby railway station, now a private dwelling, on your left. Where the river curves away to the right continue straight ahead to cross an otherwise awkward stream by a bridge. Now make your way diagonally back to the river on your right. Although this is a right of way, the path is not defined.

Now shape your course along the river's edge, going under the arch of a road bridge ahead - or across the road if flood waters prevent this - and when Kirkby Thore comes into view and you approach the confluence of Trout Beck and the Eden, ahead, go through an arch under the dismantled railway line on your left. Cross the field you are now in, aiming for the right of some bungalows ahead and go through two stiles, set apart, to the A66.

Turn right along the A66 to cross Trout Beck and immediately turn right again to go through a farmyard and along a farm road, which at first keeps close to Trout Beck on its left, then bends to the left towards a small wood ahead. Keep to the farm road, passing the edge of the wood on your right and then go through a gate on your right into a pasture, which cross diagonally back to the river on your right. The way now keeps close to the river bank, crossing stiles, all the way to Bolton bridge.

Cross the bridge and take the minor road immediately to the left, which only leads to a campsite. About 100 yards along it, on the right, there is a gate set at an angle leading into a field and a signpost indicating a footpath to New Bewley. Go through the gate and along a pasture, keeping close to the hedge on your right, to where the hedge turns sharply right. Do likewise, crossing a ditch and climbing uphill to a stile over a fence ahead. Once over the stile, climb the hill obliquely to your left, aiming for the fence running along most of the hill's top edge. Keeping close to it on your right, go along the top of the bank to where a water course bars your way. Go back down the hill, on the left bank of the water course and cross a stile at the bottom. Now turn right along the foot of the hill to a wire fence, which should have some means of getting over it, this being a signposted right of way, but hasn't.

The Eden, at the bottom of this field, has just described a broad loop, at the downstream end of which a feeder runs into it from across the field ahead.

Entry into the field is tricky because of the fence and great care must be taken to avoid damage to person or clothing by the barbed wire along the top of it. But once this barrier has been negotiated, keep close to the fence on your right and walk to where the feeder enters the field. Cross it, go through the gate on your right and a second one immediately on your left and continue along the foot of the hill to a field house clearly seen ahead. From there take the farm road which soon climbs up the hill close to a wood which covers a bank below which is the Eden. On the left, near the top of the hill, another signpost points diagonally across the field on the left which enter through a field gate and cross by first keeping close to the top of the wooded river bank, then, once a field gate and a signpost are seen to the right, diagonally to enter the Appleby to Bolton road at that point.

Turn left along this road to the beginning of Colby village where take the farm road to Colby Laithes farm, signposted, steeply downhill on the left to cross Hoff Beck over a pipe bridge. Continue along the farm road to Colby Laithes farm and when close to the farm buildings,

Watersmeet, Eden and Eamont

go through a gate on the right and uphill, along a lane edging a wood.

Within a few yards of the lane ending at a field gate go over a stile on the right and take the field track straight ahead which keeps close to a fence on the left. Soon the track turns sharp left and, keeping close to the hedge on the right, crosses fields, through gates and over stiles, to enter Banks Wood, which edges the river.

Continue straight ahead, through the wood, uphill to where the path turns right out of the wood into a field. Immediately after leaving the wood, turn left, ignoring the clear route up the field, to take a much less clearly defined one along the edge of the wood on your left. This leads into Appleby and the end of the section. (For the Ladies' Walk diversion, Langwathby to Edenhall circular, see p.110.)

The Background Story

Langwathby, "the settlement at the long ford," has had some top drawer owners. The manor, along with that of Edenhall, was bestowed by Henry I on Henry Fitz Sweyn; but not for long because the King then decided to keep it as a royal estate. King John held it, as did Henry III, who gave it to Alexander, King of Scotland, as part of 200 librates of land granted to the Scots in 1237 in return for the release of Cumberland and Westmorland. The Scottish monarch held it until the defection of John Baliol, when it reverted to the English Crown and was granted by Richard II to Ralph Neville, first Earl of Westmorland, to be held by him and his male heirs. On his death Richard Neville, "the stout Earl of Warwick" inherited it; but, in 1471 the manor again came to the Crown when Edward IV gave it to his brother, Richard, Duke of Gloucester, who became Richard III. The Crown had it until 1696 when William III granted it to William Bentinck, first Earl of Portland in whose family it remained until it was purchased by the Duke of Devonshire in 1787.

The village, sitting on a high embankment on the north bank of the Eden, surrounds a large green with the village hall at one end and The Shepherd's Inn at the other.

In 1686 a three-arched sandstone bridge was built across the Eden to link Langwathby with the tiny hamlet of Edenhall and all points to Penrith. This fine structure was washed away in one of the worst floods of 1968, to be replaced by an ugly, light controlled, one way only, metal girder bridge that is completely out of harmony with the surrounding countryside.

The "Luck of Edenhall," however, is something altogether different. It is a famous 13th century tumbler, some 6.5 inches high, made of green, specky glass. It expands in easy curves from its base upwards to end in a graceful lip enamelled with a geometrical design in crimson, blue and yellow. The tumbler is a characteristic Syrian glass of a type attributed to the once famous glass making centre of Aleppo.

The "Luck" has been protected down the centuries by a fourteenth century leather case of the highest quality which was made either in the Narbonne region of France or in England. The initials I.H.S. stamped on its lid identify it with the church and it may be that the "Luck" was a chalice used for communion. The projection of its lip makes it somewhat inconvenient as a drinking glass.

The "Luck of Edenhall" has long been associated with the Musgrave family, whose history is closely linked with that of the village. When Sir Thomas Musgrave married Joan, second daughter and co-heir of Sir William Stapleton of Edenhall, the estate came into the possession of the Musgraves; and when Sir Thomas died in 1467 his four sons and four daughters assured the Musgrave succession.

How the Musgraves came to own the "Luck" is shrouded in mystery. They were a war-like lot so it is probable that one of the family brought it back with him when he returned from the Crusades. This is the most logical explanation: yet legend has it that it was seized from the fairies by a butler at the hall who found them making merry round St. Cuthbert's Well, when he went there to fetch water. As the frightened fairies fled, one of those at the rear turned and screamed a warning.

> If that cup shall break or fall
> Farewell the Luck of Edenhall.

This had absolutely no effect on stout Philip, Duke of Wharton, a hardened drinker, who delighted, when staying at Edenhall, in tossing the "Luck" high in the air and catching it as it fell.

In 1926 the "Luck of Edenhall" was loaned to the Victoria and Albert and in 1958 the museum was fortunate enough to acquire it. So the tumbler survives.

During the Middle Ages "Luck" became associated with the cult of St. Cuthbert and Edenhall has both a well and a church dedicated to him.

As for Edenhall itself, the most recent mansion, an elegant piece of architectural splendour in the Italian style, was built around 1821 amidst glorious parkland which itself was enhanced by the meandering Eden, the lovely fourteenth century church of St. Cuthbert and, beyond, the Pennines at their highest and best. Two splendid cedars of Lebanon of great age and beauty stood watchful over a beautiful flower garden.

The hall was demolished in 1934.

The church remains and is well worth a visit. The east window is though to be a piece of Venetian work. The marble slab inside the altar rail is inlaid with two brass plates depicting Sir William Stapleton, who died in the middle of the 15th century, and his tiny wife. The church also holds the original clappers of its bells.

One lofty cedar remains: one of the tallest trees in England.

A fine circular walk maintains a link between Edenhall and Langwathby that began in 1380. It is an easy walk, some 3.5 miles long, and makes a diversion from the main route that is as bewitching as its name, Ladies' Walk.

Langwathby's village green makes a good starting point, from where the way is along the Penrith road through the "Straits," the narrow exit from the village to the river, which is crossed by the aforementioned girder bridge.

If this "temporary" bridge leaves much to be desired, the view from it can raise the spirit. Salmon spawn under it, migrating whooper swans visit the flat fields alongside it and herons roost in the trees downstream of it.

Once across the bridge, the way is through a field upstream of it, which is entered through a gap stile in a wall, signposted to Edenhall. Known as the Mains, the field is subjected to flooding after heavy rains. The path follows the river's edge, upstream, and in summer is knee-deep in Himalayan balsam, willow herb, brambles and butterbur.

At the upstream end of the field, the path turns right, away from the Eden, and heads directly for Edenhall along a ridge, sheltered for a good half of the way by a belt of Scots pine and firs, which were planted in the 1960s. Because the ridge resembles reins falling down a horse's neck it used to be called "Hanging Reins." Today, because the field on its western side is often very dry, the path is now nicknamed "The Desert Ship."

An earlier path, built in 1815 by the Musgrave family to take boys from Langwathby to school at Edenhall, went diagonally across the field from the Eden bridge to the tiny, red sandstone school at its other end which the Musgraves had also built. The school was improved as a result of the Education Act of 1870 and in 1874 girls from an earlier village school moved into the new school with the boys. Meanwhile, in 1867 a school opened in Langwathby so there was a fall in the number of pupils attending Edenhall school.

From the old school-house Ladies' Walk turns left to the war memorial from where there is an extensive view of the village. Along the road to the right are to be found, in quick succession, a long house converted from a tithe barn, tall Edenhall Farm house which was built in the 1770s and later became known as Home Farm, the courtyard with its clocktower, which used to be the stables for the Hall. The man who designed this elegant edifice was Sir Robert Smirke (1781-1867) who also designed the Hall. He also designed the British Museum.

Not far from the clocktower two pairs of semi-detached houses, called Beaconsfield Terrace, display the Musgrave Arms which incorporate the red hand of Ulster. Apparently, this was granted to the family in recognition of their services to the province.

Until the 1870s the villagers used to play quoits on a wide area of common land across the road from the Hall. But the Lady of the Manor disapproved of the noise so close to her home and had the common land enclosed, which, apart from being illegal, was not nice. The quoiting pitch was moved to another site close to where the present war memorial stands. It was called Potters' Garth because itinerant tinkers and potters frequently encamped there. Whenever they came to Edenhall these travellers caused great excitement among the villagers because they brought with them the latest news from the outside world. But Lady Musgrave did not approve and had this further piece of common land enclosed.

Such overbearing arrogance, such a lack of understanding of the needs of ordinary folk, placed that particular Lady Musgrave firmly at the bottom of Edenhall's popularity stakes. By abusing her position, the wretched woman had deprived the villagers of what was rightly theirs and in so doing had lost the esteem of a community.

The way left from the war memorial is along Church Lane, which leads to St. Cuthbert's very old and very lovely church, much of which dates from the 12th century. The church stands in solitary splendour inside the old deer park; and, soon after passing through the park gateway, Ladies' Walk splits. Just beyond this parting of the ways, close to the path leading to the church, stands the Plague Cross on the site of a basin which contained vinegar. Victims of the plague used to place money into the vinegar: money to pay for the food brought by people from Penrith. Some of them lived in shacks clustered around the church and others on the fells to where they had fled when the plague - probably typhus rather than bubonic - hit the village in the late 16th century killing a quarter of the inhabitants.

There used to be a wall around the churchyard but it was removed in the 1870s by order of Lady Musgrave and the stone used to build the retaining wall of the Ladies' Walk proper.

St. Cuthbert's church never fails to impress. On the western face of its 15th century tower, which was a place of refuge during the border raids, are four carved shields representing the arms of Musgraves, Veteriponts, Stapletons and Hiltons, four important families who histories are linked to that of Edenhall.

Once archery was practised in the churchyard and the grooves in the stonework at the eastern end of the church were probably made by archers sharpening their arrows. Yews for making bows were planted in the churchyard, safely out of reach of livestock to which whey were poisonous. In the 1800s, when deer were introduced to Edenhall, the yews were removed.

Having inspected the church retrace steps to the Plague Cross and take the path that makes an oblique right turn to the Eden and that part of the walk from which its name is derived.

A tall iron gate in a deer-proof fence on the river bank used to mark the upstream access to Ladies' Walk proper. It was to this pleasant spot that the Musgrave ladies came in their carriages to walk the broad path and be collected at the other end, having sauntered through a delight of mixed woodland.

Today a kissing gate on the river bank is the upstream entrance to

Ladies' Walk. The hazels, the ashes, beeches and sycamore are still there, as are the celandines in springtime, the forget-me-knots a littler later on and, in summer, lords and ladies, bellflowers, violets and wild garlic. But parts of the walk have collapsed, thanks to the removal of the willows which once grew along the river's rim, binding the banks with their roots and absorbing surplus water like blotting paper, so keeping the river bank in good condition.

Perhaps one day this still delightful walk will be restored to its former glory. For it has so much to offer: in later summer, large concentrations of curlews and oystercatchers and, all the year round, superb views of Cross Fell, the highest part of the Pennines.

Progressing downstream, the roof-tops of Langwathby come into view on the other side of the river. Then comes the bridge and in next to no time a return to Langwathby.

* * *

Culgaith straggles the top of "T Pea" which is the name given to the hill through which the Settle–Carlisle line passes along a tunnel 600 yards long. This hill is one of three things for which the village used to be famous, the others being its brass band and Atkinson's sausages, now no longer made there. The village church of All Saints was built in 1756 on the site of an older one. There are no stained glass windows in it, which is unusual for so old an Anglican place of worship. The Wesleyan chapel, dated 1830, is still in use, as is The Black Swan.

Behind Culgaith the Pennines sweep magnificently to the skyline while to westward, across the valley, Saddleback and other eastern fells gladden the eye.

One of the feeders tumbling from the high Pennines is Crowdundle Beck which, on its journey to the Eden, flows through lovely oak woods to the rear and side of Acorn Bank.

Acorn Bank, originally called Sowerby Manor, was first occupied during the early years of the 12th century by warrior monks known as The Knights Templars. This order, which was established for the defence of the Holy Sepulchre and the protection of Christian pilgrims, gradually became mercenary and in 1312 it was suppressed. But the link lives on in the name of the nearby village: Temple Sowerby, "a farmstead on sour land owned by The Knights Templars."

The Eden upstream of Bolton

In 1323 the possessions of The Knights Templars were given to the Knights Hospitalers - The Knights of St. John of Jerusalem - and so Sowerby Manor came into the care of a band of brothers who cultivated crops and helped the community.

When in 1543, the Church refused to allow Henry VIII to take another wife and he reacted by disbanding all the religious houses, he granted the manor of Temple Sowerby to the landowning Dalston family, whose descendants, a century later, enclosed the gardens in the fashion of the time. The Dalstons lived at Acorn Bank for many years until the Boazmans from County Durham became the new owners through marriage.

In 1930 Kenneth Boazman sold Acorn Bank, the mill and 120 acres of land to Captain and Mrs McGregor Phillips.

Mrs Phillips was the well known Yorkshire Dales poetess and authoress, Dorothy Una Ratcliffe. She wrote many of her books at Acorn Bank.

A keen naturalist, Dorothy Una Ratcliffe started a wild flower and bird reserve behind the manor which became a winter habitat for wild ducks. Badgers and otters lived there among the 65 different varieties of daffodils, including Wordsworth's small, wild Lenten Lily, which she planted. In 1950 she presented Acorn Bank to the National Trust.

In 1976 the Sue Ryder Foundation became the tenant of Acorn Bank and set about converting it for its present purpose, a home for those elderly and disabled people who can no longer manage in their own homes and have no families to look after them. As near as possible to a home in the real sense, it has 24 beds, and a warm-hearted, dedicated staff.

The garden is run by the National Trust and has one of the most extensive herb gardens in the country. It is open to the public.

Crowdundle Beck meets the Eden well to the north of Temple Sowerby.

Our route, across fields and along a quiet minor road from the front of Acorn Bank, goes right through the middle of this pretty village.

Kirkby Thore is pleasantly sited near the confluence of the Eden and Trout Beck on the site of the Roman camp, *Bravoniacum* close to where Maiden Way branched from the Roman road from York to Carlisle. Despite its name, the village has no connection with the god

Wharton Hall in Mallerstang
Photo: Walt Unsworth   113

Thor. The name is derived from the Norse *thor* and the Hiberno-Celtic *tochar* meaning highway. It is the Roman road that gives Kirkby Thore its name.

The first recorded lord of the manor of Kirkby Thore was a knight called Whelp and it is probably from him that Whelp Castle got its name. He lived there during the lawless days of King Stephen's reign.

Today Kirkby Thore, which lies mainly to the north of the A66, is home to many workers of a nearby plaster works. Its church is dedicated to St. Michael. The church bell, which was cast at York in 1450, is probably the largest in the old county of Westmorland. There is a Methodist church, which was built in 1829 as a Wesleyan chapel. The pub at the south end of the village is The Bridge End Inn, probably named after the bridge carrying the A66 over Trout Beck.

The Eden, running smooth and deep past Kirkby Thore, is much favoured by anglers. No hedges embroider its grassy banks, neither dry stone wall nor wire fence impede access to the brown waters and no overhanging branches poise to snag a cast. In short, there is nothing to distract an honest fisherman in the serious business of landing a whopper!

To many anglers the eagerly sought after whopper is the salmon, the most magical fish of all. It is a mystery that one is caught at all by fly fishers for salmon returning to their spawning beds do not eat, relying on their fat to sustain them. Salmon snap at a fly either out of irritation or playfulness, tackling anything one day, ignoring everything the next, favouring large, gaudy ones sometimes, at others switching their attentions to small subdued ones. Their behaviour is consistent only in its inconsistency. Frustrating, yes; but, as one dedicated angler told me, all part and parcel of a good day's fishing.

A little way upstream of Kirkby Thore the river bank once more becomes tree-lined and remains so all the way to Bolton bridge and beyond. The roots bind the banks, the trunks harbour cities of insects, birds nest in the branches and summer foliage gives shade.

The village of Bolton, whose name means the place of dwellings, stands back from the river, uphill from the bridge. It is picturesque and friendly despite a tombstone at its church of All Saints which carries a skull and crossbones. The church is mainly Norman and six-petalled rosettes and figured capitals pattern its doorway. Above a north window, which was once a Norman doorway, there is a slab which shows a carving of two knights jousting. A poor box, on the right just inside the church, is dated 1634. The font cover, on the left as you go in, is dated 1687. The chancel arch has a lovely carved screen.

On lonely Maulds Meaburn Moor, some six miles south-west of Appleby-in-Westmorland, Dry Beck springs to life. Scale Beck is born a little further south, on Bank Moor. For close on three miles these infant streams retain their separate identities, then join to become Hoff Beck, which meanders in a most delightful way northwards to feed the Eden near Colby. Just short of a mile after the meeting of Dry Beck and Scale Beck, this lively stream plunges over Rutter Falls, a sheer drop of about twenty feet which, when in spate, is most impressive.

A footbridge a couple of hundred yards below the falls, alongside a ford, is a good vantage point.

Throughout its length Hoff Beck snakes through rich farmland along a bedrock not of red sandstone as you would expect in the Eden Valley, but of limestone.

The only places, apart from farms, it flows past on its way to the Eden are the hamlet of Hoff and the village of Colby, where it is known by the locals as Colby Beck.

The "hill farmstead," Colby, was held by a family bearing the local name from the reign of Henry II to that of Richard II when it passed by an heiress to the Warcops who held it from 1402 until the Restoration when most of the tenements were "sold to freehold." The village stands on raised ground about one and a quarter miles west by north of Appleby.

At one time you could walk from Colby to Appleby by a very pleasant, roundabout route by way of Colby Laithes Farm, crossing the Eden there on stepping-stones and reaching the town along the river's eastern bank. But countless floods first weakened then washed away these stepping-stones, effectively terminating this walk at the water's edge. So a new and equally pleasant way was developed, an airy route that had no need to cross the river. At first it keeps away from the Eden, going uphill along a lane, then crossing fields, returning to the river at Banks Wood and staying close to it all the way to Appleby.

The Cloisters at Appleby

8:   Appleby to Warcop

Length of section:	7 miles
Total distance:	58 miles
Map:	O.S. Landranger 91
Handy hostelry:	The Chamley Arms.

Route Directions

From St. Lawrence's church walk straight ahead, up Boroughgate, until close to the main entrance to the castle grounds, where follow the road, Scattergate, to the right, which keeps alongside the perimeter wall of the castle as it descends. At the bottom of the hill, keep close to the castle wall, passing cottages on your right, to where the road bends sharply to the right. Here take the road which continues straight ahead, steeply downhill to the Eden. At the bottom of the hill take the path on your right and continue along it, upstream, at a tangent and it will bring you to the river bank.

Continue upstream for about a mile to where, immediately beyond a narrow feeder, a stile is crossed. Once over it ignore the more obvious track left to the riverside and turn right for a few yards to where the trees on your left end. There turn left, climb the bank and continue along the top of the wooded bank edging the Eden along a clear track.

Where, ahead, a stream flows into the Eden through a steep, wooded ghyll, climb the stile into the wood, go down the path to cross the stream on a footbridge and climb the other side, still on the path. Go through the gate ahead and continue, out of the wood, to the top of the field. There go through the gate on your left and over the brow of the rising land towards where the Settle-Carlisle line cuts across your line of walk on an embankment. Go through an underpass, clearly seen and along the lane at the far side which will bring you to Ormside.

Turn left towards Great Ormside Hall, then right, along a tarmac road, first going uphill, then bending to the right, to Little Ormside. Once past Little Ormside the road becomes a lane, crosses a ford, climbs a steep hill and levels out. Then it makes a very severe right

<u>Appleby to Warcop</u>

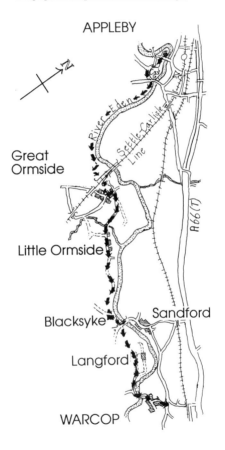

turn. Here continue straight ahead through a gate and across a field towards the river on a broad farm track. As it closes on the river it climbs a hill to get close to it at the top of a high, wooded bank. A gate on the left leads into this wood at the top of the bank. Go through it and take the path downhill, through the wood to Blacksyke Farm.

The way is now through the farmyard and down the lane to where a bridge crosses the Eden. There you will see a stile on the river bank, on the right-hand side, immediately before the bridge. Cross it and continue upstream along the river bank (with permission from Blacksyke Farm) for a good mile to join the farm road from Langford Farm, always in view on your right. The farm road leads to a lane which will bring you downhill to where a beautiful stone bridge spans the Eden. Cross the bridge and follow the road into Warcop and the end of the section.

(The official route, once you have crossed the riverside stile near Blacksyke is right and uphill, behind some cottages and a hedge on your right. At the top of the hill go through a gate into the field on your right. Continue ahead, keeping close to the fence, now on your left, turning left when it does. Ahead there is a gate leading, end on,

Warcop bridge 16th century. The only bridge across the Eden to withstand the floods of 1822

into a lane. Go through it and down the lane which will bring you to the lovely stone bridge over the Eden and to the end of the section.)

The Background Story

Appleby Grammar School *amo, amo* and I hope *amatis* too. Good old A.G.S. where for five gloriously happy, informative years, dedicated teachers of considerable ability strove to instil into me - and other *puerile ignorami* - the mysteries of learning, thus continuing a tradition of scholastic excellence that had its foundation on the west side of Kirkgate - today's Low Wiend - in 1453.

It was in a building adjoining St. Lawrence's church at Kirkgate, called "School House Lane," that the chantry priest of Appleby was enjoined to teach at a free grammar school in the borough as part of his duty; and the first recorded headmaster was Thomas Whinfell (1478). This state of affairs continued until the suppression of the monasteries.

The school was refounded in 1574 when Queen Elizabeth I granted it a Charter and in 1887 a new school was erected to supersede the old buildings, which were condemned after centuries of use. An elegant sandstone building, it is sited to the north of the town a little way

Settle -Carlisle line crossing the Eden near Ormside

beyond the summit of a steep hill called Battlebarrow and set back from the left-hand side of the road behind a spacious lawn and rose beds.

A.G.S. has expanded since I was there and is now a co-educational grammar school. Its new buildings include an arts and crafts room, a biology lab., a domestic science room and a woodwork room. It now caters for all children of secondary school age from Appleby and the surrounding district.

Across the road from the grammar school entrance, the Settle-Carlisle line approaches Appleby station from the north-west along a high embankment, having kept to the Eden Valley proper all the way from Carlisle. Now, for its long climb to Ais Gill summit, although continuing to follow the river, it does so from a more elevated course through wild, mountainous scenery that warms the heart and makes the adrenalin flow.

It is at Appleby that the Settle-Carlisle throws out a loop to the truncated Eden Valley line which, in its day, linked Penrith and Darlington. Between Cliburn and Kirkby Stephen this scenic run was never far from the Eden. Today the only part of it still used is the section between Appleby's link with the Settle-Carlisle and Warcop, where the Army has a permanent camp and an important firing range. Had it not been for the demands of the Army, this length of track would have gone the way the rest of the line.

Appleby, "farmstead with an apple tree," was renamed Appleby-in-Westmorland when that proud county was merged with Cumberland to form Cumbria. It is beautifully situated in two parishes with the Eden between them. The greater part of the town lies in the parish of St. Lawrence on the river's left bank: St. Michael, popularly called Bongate, "street of peasant landowners or unfree tenants," and much the smaller parish of the two, is on its right bank.

People have lived there for over a thousand years yet history is entirely silent about its early days. Of all the settlements in the Eden Valley, it is one of the youngest. Where, on the limestone uplands between Shap and Crosby Garrett Neolithic barrows, Bronze Age cairns, stone circles and pre-Roman villages abound, none is to be found at Appleby. Nor would any be expected to be, because in Neolithic times the valley bottom was carpeted with swamps and impenetrable forest.

The Romans had camps at *Verterae,* (Brough), and *Braboniacum,* (Kirkby Thore), but none in between, although the road joining the camps ran through the eastern part of Appleby, which would imply that the place was of little importance to them.

In the 6th century the Anglo-Saxons subdued the post-Roman Celtic population. They in turn, were subdued by the Danes, who invaded the Eden Valley from the west in the 10th century and settled there. They were Appleby's first settlers. Under the Danes it became a place of some importance, giving its name to one of the shires, Appleby-scire, into which Westmorland was divided.

In the 11th century Anglo-Saxon rule was re-established for a short time but by the time William the Conqueror had landed at Pevensey and defeated and killed Harold at Hastings in 1066 the district had become part of the Scottish Kingdom. For that reason Appleby was never occupied by the Normans and does not appear in the Domesday Book. Not until 1092, when William Rufus marched on Carlisle with a large army and added Cumberland and Westmorland to his dominions did Appleby return to English rule: not until then did Appleby's written history begin.

William II granted the Barony of Westmorland to Ranulf de Meschines, who began building castles at Appleby and Brough. As the seat of the Barony, Appleby became the County Town, gaining a dignity it maintained until 1175 when William the Lion, King of Scotland, arrived unexpectedly with an army and destroyed the town before taking Brough by storm and doing considerable damage throughout the countryside.

According to Jordon Fantesme, a contemporary recorder "the King (of Scotland) very soon had the castle of Appleby : there were no people in it, it was quite unguarded. Gospatric, son of Orme, an old grey-headed Englishman, was constable and he soon cried mercy."

For his conduct Gospatric was fined 500 marks by King Henry II and his subordinate officers in sums varying according to their rank. After this episode, by order of the King, the castle was strengthened and the town rebuilt.

In 1179 Henry II granted the Burgesses of Appleby a Charter conferring on them the same privileges as were enjoyed by the people of York. These were extended by King John, who was at Appleby on June 18th and 19th, 1212. He bestowed on the burgesses the town itself, giving them control over local government and freeing them from feudal impositions. King John also granted the town its present arms of "thee lions passant guardant in pale, or, crowned with ducal coronets of the last."

For the succeeding century and a half Appleby prospered and expanded. Under Henry III it had a mayor and two provosts; and during the reign of Edward II it was paying a fee farm rent of twenty marks a year, equal to 2,200 burgages, from which the population at that time can be estimated at upwards of 11,000 folk.

But early in the 14th century the Scots became troublesome once more, burning the town in 1314 and attacking it again in 1319. Although Appleby overcame these blows it never recovered from the devastating surprise attack on St. Stephen's day, 1388, when, once again, it was laid waste by the Scots. In consequence it was unable to pay the fee farm rent due to the Crown and its pristine splendour and importance was lost for ever.

The old borough boundary is at Burrells, a mile from the present town, and the foundations of buildings ploughed up in fields between two and three miles of Boroughgate are evidence of Appleby's size before that ferocious St. Stephen's day raid. So devastating was it that as late as 1515 it was recorded that "the town of *Apulbye* is greatly diminished and fallen into ruin..... having been burnt by the Scots in the year of Our Lord 1388 and never from the same time until now rebuilt, but the greater part of the same town as yet lies in ruins."

In 1598 the plague raged at Appleby with such severity that its market was removed to Gilhaughlin, near Cliburn. Not only was the place down: it was almost out.

During the Civil War, because the people of Appleby remained loyal to the King, Cromwell imposed upon the town a "Charter of Restrictions." When it arrived neither the mayor nor the bailiffs would read it and the soldiery "had to have recourse unto a fellow in the market, an unclean bird, hatched at Kirkby Stephen, the nest of all traitors, who proclaimed it aloud."

A garrison of Roundheads was stationed there for a time to ensure that the Charter was enforced.

It was annulled on the restoration of Charles II, an event that was celebrated in the town with great pomp and festivity under the auspices of the remarkable Lady of the Manor, the Lady Anne

Clifford, Countess Dowager of Pembroke, Dorset and Montgomery and High Sheriffess by inheritance of the County of Westmorland. In 1648 she had fortified the castle for Charles I and encouraged the besieged garrison to hold out until provisions failed. Now, although an old lady, with the restoration of the monarchy, she "thought not her gates too wide to receive her guests."

Lady Anne is best remembered for the large sums she spent rebuilding the Clifford family castles at Appleby, Brough, Brougham, Skipton and Pendragon and restoring churches in all these places. She is also remembered for the bridges she built, the alms houses she endowed and her concern for the well-being of her tenants. She died in 1675 "at her castle at Brougham, Christianly, willingly and quietly." She is buried at Appleby in St. Lawrence's church.

The cloisters of St. Lawrence's church mark the bottom end of Appleby's main street, Boroughgate, at the other end of which, on a lofty eminence, stands the castle. Just outside the cloisters there is an 18th century pillar known as the Low Cross, with a similar, older one gracing the top end, outside the castle gates. This one carries the inscription:

> Retain your loyalty,
> Preserve your rights.

The wide, bottom end of Boroughgate is the market place, in the middle of which, opposite the Tufton Arms, there is a bull ring let into a stone, a survival of bull baiting with dogs prior to slaughter, which was supposed to improve the quality of the meat.

The block of buildings of indeterminate age squatting in the middle of Boroughgate close to the foot of its climb to the castle is the Moot Hall where, in an upper storey, four aldermen and twelve councillors would deal with the borough's business.

One of these aldermen, who became Mayor of Appleby before his meteoric career propelled him to a more elevated station in life, was Jack Robinson, son of an Appleby shopkeeper, who was educated at Appleby Grammar School before being apprenticed to an attorney. Sir James Lowther, first Earl of Lonsdale, took him into his employment and discovered that he had an unusual aptitude for maths. Under Sir James's patronage Jack Robinson's rise was rapid. He became M.P. for Westmorland and afterwards for the Borough of Harwich, Lieutenant-Colonel of the Westmorland Militia, Secretary of the

Treasury and, lastly, Surveyor-General of His Majesty's Woods and Forests. He became a great friend of King George III.

In 1763, when he became M.P. for Westmorland, Jack Robinson rebuilt the house known today as the "White House" midway along Boroughgate, on the left as you climb towards the High Cross at its southern end. It was there that he entertained his friends lavishly, including Lord North, the Prime Minister. The house is better known as "the house that Jack built." Jack Robinson is also credited with building High Cross. Despite his meteoric rise to fame the phrase "as soon as you can say Jack Robinson" does not refer to him despite convenient legends. According to Burke, it was found in books before he was born.

The main gates of Appleby castle are just beyond High Cross at the top of Boroughgate and there is another entrance in Scattergate. The noble pile itself is magnificently situated on a knoll that on one side falls headlong into the Eden. It is a typical early Norman motte and bailey castle surrounded by a ditch some 30 feet deep in places. Its sits in the middle of Appleby's first castle, one of the largest earthworks in Britain, which was thrown up by Ranulph de Meschines to strengthen a naturally defensive site.

A superb Norman keep, "Caesar's Tower," which stands at the western end of the castle on the motte, was probably built in the late 12th century and heightened after the surrender of the garrison to William the Lion and his Scots in the summer of 1174. In the 17th century Lady Anne Clifford restored and internally altered it, leaving intact the original stone staircase leading to the roof, which commands extensive views over the surrounding countryside, including, on the edge of town to the N.N.E., just beyond the bypass, rising heathland known as Gallows Hill. The castle is a Rare Breed Survival Trust Centre and is open to the public from Easter to September.

Gallows Hill is less famed for the gibbet, which once stood there, than for its long association with Appleby Fair, one of the two largest gypsy fairs in the north of England: Brough Hill Fair at Warcop is the other. In June, 1985 Appleby Fair celebrated its 300th anniversary, having existed since 1685 under the protection of a charter granted by James II. About 1750 its date was moved forward by one week to its present one and its title altered to Appleby New Fair. It is thought that this came about because in 1752 the Georgian calendar came into being with the consequent alteration of dates.

Until about 1830 Gallows Hill was outside the Appleby parish boundary. In 1911 the heath was enclosed and the gypsies parked their vardos, wagons and caravans and set up camps along the verges of the adjoining by-roads. The second Tuesday and Wednesday of June are the main fair days but these colourful travelling folk - true Romany didakai (half-breed gypsies), mumpers (low class van dwellers not of Romany blood) and itinerant gorgios (non-gypsies) - begin arriving several days prior to the Fair's official opening. It regularly attracts about five hundred people, making it the largest gathering of gypsy and travelling folk in Britain. For many it is their annual holiday and all are intent on enjoying themselves and doing a fair amount of trade.

Of course, whenever large numbers of people gather together there is always a small minority ready to cause offence and Appleby New Fair is no exception. So some of the town's shopkeepers shut-up shop for the duration and publicans remove from their bars any items likely to be "lifted." Not that this worries the travelling folk who spend enough cash in the local pubs in a week to pay for the rates of the premises for twelve months.

In 1965, when the Fair was seriously threatened with closure, Gordon Boswell, representing the gypsy people, led and spoke for a deputation that saved this historic gathering. From the outset he had problems because he and his supporters were unable to find the original charter. Furthermore, when the New Fair was given the mayoral seal of approval in 1750 no charter could be found for this either.

Nevertheless, Boswell impressed everyone at the council meeting with his honesty and determination. He arranged for a collection of well over £100 from the travellers to pay for the tidying up of the site when they had left. The money was lodged with a Catholic priest, Father Caton, who had to pay the contractor once the area had been left tidy.

At a further meeting, with the approval of the Mayor of Appleby and the support of the Chairman of the Health and Highways Committee, it was agreed that the Fair should continue.After many further meetings it was also agreed that the enclosed thirty acres of Gallows Hill would become the camping area, leaving the adjacent by-roads clear. The council would provide water points and latrines and each traveller would pay £2 to a special Appleby Fair Fund which would be paid to the council in return for their facilities. The gypsies would also refrain from running and trading their horses in the town centre.

So every June, "Fair Hill," as everyone calls it, and the adjacent roads and lanes, hum with activity. Horse-drawn units are outnumbered these days by opulent motor-drawn caravans; but it is the old vardos that attract most attention. Reading wagons, named after the area where they were first made and the most beautiful of the Romany caravans, are seldom seen at Appleby. But Bow Tops, that have a style most favoured by the gypsies, are there every year, as are the open Lot wagons which are still made today.

Anyone passing the living trailers of the itinerants cannot fail to be impressed by the beautiful bone china and the very best of Waterford glassware so proudly displayed. The china is usually Royal Crown Derby with the Japan Amari patterns in rich blues, reds and gold being the most popular. About the turn of the century the gypsies collected Royal Crown Derby because it was so cheap to buy. Down the years its bright and colourful designs became associated with travelling folk. Today it is far from cheap but is still collected by travellers, many of whom call at the factory in Derby to make their purchases en route to Appleby.

At the Fair china and glassware stalls do brisk business, gypsy women make and sell cushions and children's dresses, using the brightest of materials and fortune-tellers are ever eager to read a palm or a tea leaf. Most claim relationship to Gypsy Rose Lee or Petulengro, which is the gypsy name for Smith. Fortune-tellers appear to have increased in number down the years, few, as the wags would have it, having gone out of business due to unforeseen circumstances!

Prior to being offered for sale, many of the horses are bathed in the Eden, washing-up liquid by the plastic container full providing the lather. This may improve the look of the horses but the effect on the fish is disastrous.

Appleby New Fair, then, is an ambivalence; but, for all its shortcomings, life would be the duller without it. It is a meeting of different cultures, a rich anachronism, an escape from humdrum urbanity, an adventure. Long may it remain. Somehow I think it will, for as Ron Finch puts it in his evocative poem on the subject:

> Appleby Fair will always be there
> The gypsies will keep it forever
> Locked and sealed in their care.

Between Appleby and Great Ormside the Eden flows smoothly along its sandstone bed, its surface unruffled by rocky outcrops and gravelly shallows. Appleby Angling Association has the fishing rights but this does not deter herons and poachers from helping themselves. Canoeists find it to their liking and the riverside walk is a delight.

At the Great Ormside end of it, the village is approached through an underpass on the Settle-Carlisle line mid-way between where it crosses the Eden on a ten-arched viaduct and the now-closed Ormside station. Ormside was one of the least important stations on the line and never generated much traffic.

The village is gathered comfortably around its triangular green, exuding quiet contentment. Some of its farms are 17th century and its church, on a hill close to the Eden, is a scheduled monument, having been a place for burial and worship for some 2,000 years. There is a short, square base to its gabled roof but it has neither spire nor tower: nor does it have any stained glass. But near the altar rail there is a leper's squint. The church is dedicated to St. James and is reached through the yard of a farm which was formerly Ormside Hall.

It is thought that Ormside, "Orm's hill or headland," is named after Orm the Viking, governor of Appleby castle and father of Gospatric, though there is no evidence of this. However there is no doubt about Ormside's Viking connection. In 1899 a hoard of Viking weapons was found there and is now in Carlisle Museum. In 1823 a ninth century gold and silver cup was found in Ormside churchyard. Named the Ormside Cup, it is now in York Museum.

An Ormside priest called John is said to have drawn-up the will of the Black Prince.

From the north end of Great Ormside a quiet road leads, first eastwards, then curving, S.S.E., to the tiny hamlet of Little Ormside and continues as a narrow lane to Hemels, an isolate farm. Both quiet road and narrow lane are roughly parallel to and seldom further than

Near The Thrang, Mallerstang

Stenkrith, near Kirkby Stephen

The Nine Standards seen from the summit of the Rigg
Photo: Walt Unsworth

a field away from the Eden. Within half a mile of Hemels the lane is quitted for a broad track through a field that brings us close to the river, all the way to Blacksyke, where it is crossed.

Sandford, named after a nearby sandy ford over the Eden, is not much larger today than it was in Roman times. Close to the village and not far from the A66, the old Roman road, are three tumuli, two about 270 feet in circumference and the third half that size. When one of the larger ones was opened in 1766, some human remains and an iron urn were found. All are thought to have belonged to a British chief.

The first recorded owner of the Manor of Sandford was William, son of Robert de Sandford, who gave Sandford wood and all the turbary of the township to Robert de Veteripont in return for his discharge from homage and service, ten marks of silver and one palfrey. Later the same Robert de Veteripont gave it all back to William's son, Robert de Sandford, for £20. The Sandfords hung onto it for several generations; but there came a time when all the heirs were daughters who, through marriage, passed it on to the Berdesey and Warcop families. Soon the Warcops took possession of the entire manor. But their ownership was short-lived, for, once again, their heirs were all girls and once again, through marriage, the manor was split, never to be restored to one family ownership.

The western end of the village is draped over a hillside from the top of which the vast panorama of the steep, western escarpment of the Pennine chain is seen to advantage. There, spread out in all their grandeur are the highest and most dramatic of the Pennine fells. To the distant north Cross Fell, the Fiend's Fell of old, caps the lot. Then come the twin cones of Little and Great Dun Fell, the latter with its weather station, and the stony Knock Fell, threaded together with the Pennine Way, undefined thereabouts. Then the great bite of High Cup, with its Nick, then Hilton Gill with broad Murton Fell between. Now come those fells best seen from Sandford: from west to east are Roman, Long and Middle fells followed by Helbeck Wood and Helbeck Fell.

Roman Fell is a corruption of Rutman Fell and has no connection with Romans. Helbeck is another misnomer. The old spelling was Hellebeck, meaning "a small, rapid river" and referred to Swindal Beck.

The steep escarpment of Murton Fell contains a conical eminence called Murton Pike. It is dwarfed by two nearby conical outliers, the nearer, higher one being Dufton Pike, Knock Pike is the other. These outliers and all the aforementioned fells share a unique phenomenon, the only wind in Britain to have a name of its own: the Helm Wind.

Always a violent wind, the Helm is especially strong in the late spring and autumn. Its range is confined to that part of the Pennines between Brampton in Gilsland and Brough. When a Helm is "on" its presence can be seen as well as felt because of the conditions that bring it about. First, a long, thick, white cloud, the Helm Cloud, forms along the top of the Pennines. While this is happening another parallel line of cloud, this one dark and swirling forms an almost stationary band at a distance of three or four miles from the foot of the range. This is called the Helm Bar. It is between these two banks of cloud that the Helm Wind blows with such fury. Bitterly cold, it rushes down the escarpment, gradually losing power until, when it is almost under the bar, or burr, it suddenly ceases. Since the bar forms above the Eden, the river is never crossed by the wind.

By its very nature the Helm is a destructive wind, especially in the spring following a spell of mild weather when crops have grown rapidly and there is every prospect of an early summer. Within a few hours of it rising, all the new vegetation will have been withered by its icy breath. Even in mid-summer, after a hot day, if there has been thunder about (not necessarily in the district), the Helm may rise and blow for many hours, destroying plant life, pulling leaves off trees, causing grazing animals to shiver and, sometimes, driving them headlong before it. A hail-laden springtime Helm has often been the cause of deaths among young lambs.

The only time the Helm is of benefit to the farmer is when it blows during a wet haytime or harvest when, within a few hours, it will dry out sodden hay or corn, making it fit for gathering.

Once it starts there is no telling when it will stop. Sometimes it will blow for three days but it could last for three weeks, stopping as suddenly as it starts. While the Helm is "on" it can be heard miles away, roaring in its fury, while there is not even a gentle breeze in the rest of the valley. Also, while it blows the space between the Helm Cloud and the Helm Bar is usually clear, although the rest of the sky may be cloudy. Clearly, the Helm Wind is something very special indeed.

There is a Royal Armoured Corps firing range at Warcop. Building began in 1942, F.W.Chandler of Blackpool being the construction firm with the Pioneer Corps supplying some of the labour. Three reinforced concrete, triangular circuits were constructed from where, at any given angle, tanks can fire at one-mile-distant moving targets. In another part of the range, under simulated war-like conditions, modern tracked fighting vehicles blast away at obsolete tanks which have been towed to selected sites on the steep escarpment. The whole range is a danger area and out of bounds to the general public. The troops using the range live in a hutted camp in Warcop Hall Park, across the A66 from the range, in Warcop village itself.

When approached from Sandford, the first buildings of the straggle that is Warcop are, on the left, Warcop Hall, set back on raised ground, and, on the right, edging the Eden, the church and the village school.

The church, which is dedicated to St. Columba, is Early English. After the Reformation it was sold to the Warcops and remained attached to the manor until 1957 when it was given by the then owners to the Bishop of Carlisle. The churchyard is entered through a lych-gate erected to the memory of Captain Henry Preston who was killed in the Crimea.

The old English festival, rushbearing, usually took place in the old days on the festival of the saint to whom the church was dedicated. With Warcop it was different because, although the church was dedicated to St. Columba, the festival has always been held on June 29th, St. Peter's day. The reason may be that it was fixed during the early days of Christianity to be as near as possible to some great heathen gatherings. The fact that there are some Druidic remains in the parish adds substance to this theory. For it was the policy of the ancient Christians to consider the feelings of the people they were converting. It was perfectly lawful to change a heathen gathering into a Christian festival and much better than trying to abolish it altogether.

Nowadays rushbearing at Warcop is still commemorated, with the boys bringing crosses made from rushes to St. Columba and the girls, known as "crown bearers," carrying garlands of flowers. Preceded by a band, they march in procession through the village to the church, where a service is held. During it the girls proceed in pairs to the altar steps and offer their "crowns" to the vicar who stacks them at each side of the altar. The boys then do likewise with their rushes.

Apart from Warcop, only two old Westmorland villages celebrate rushbearing; Musgrave and Ambleside.

The village pub was formerly The Railway Inn but is now called The Chamley Arms.

9: Warcop to Kirkby Stephen

Length of section:	8 miles
Total distance:	66 miles
Map:	O.S. Landranger 91
Handy Hostelries:	Black Bull, Croglin, King's Arms, Pennine, White Lion. Numerous cafés.

Route Directions

Leave Warcop from the middle of the village, first crossing the bridge over a stream then turning right along the Blea Tarn road with the stream, to begin with, on your right. Continue through the village along the road which now leaves the stream, turning left, then right, to cross the Eden, at the end of it, on a lovely stone bridge.

At the far side of the bridge immediately turn left, through a stile, and follow the riverbank upstream. Where the river curves away to the left continue straight ahead along a clear track at the end of which take a rather muddy, broad lane downhill, where cross a stream on a bridge and immediately go left by the side of a house to join a concrete road. This farm road leads from Ploughlands Farm, on your left, to Little Musgrave. Go along it to the village where turn left, passing the road end to Soulby on your right and at the end of Little Musgrave, take a very ill-defined route over rough waste ground on your left to a stile in a hedge, which cross. Go over the field ahead, bearing to the left towards the river, which you reach at the foot of a steep bank. Follow the riverbank past the remains of the Eden Valley Railway bridge and join the road from Great Musgrave to Kirkby Stephen ahead. Turn right along it for two miles, passing, after 0.25 of a mile, the Little Musgrave road end on your right and after a further mile, a narrow lane to Winton on your left and crossing the Eden at Blands Wath en route.

Once across the second bridge over the Eden, turn left and follow the river bank upstream, passing East Field Falls. Because of the course of the river the way is a dog's leg and brings you back to the road near some bungalows. Return to the road through a gate and

Warcop to Kirkby Stephen

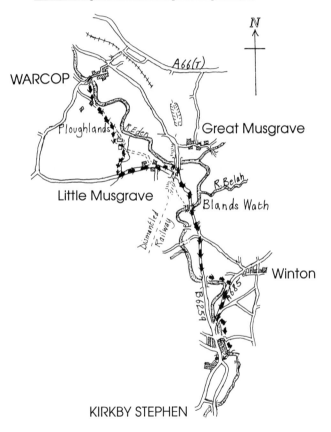

continue along it, with the river on your left to join the Brough to Kirkby Stephen road, where turn left over a bridge, cross the road and continue upstream with the river now on your right.

Where the riverside path joins the road to Hartley as its bridges the river, keep to the same side of the river. Where the road bends away from the river at Low Mill go straight ahead along a riverside footpath to Franks' Bridge, which cross. The way is now up some stone steps and right, then left to Kirkby Stephen market square and the end of the section.

The Background Story

Once an ancient cross stood on Warcop green. The base, in the form of five square steps, is still there but the cross has gone, replaced by a tall maypole topped by a pheasant wind vane.

Warcop's lovely sixteenth century bridge over the Eden fared rather better than its cross. When the severe floods of 1822 caused such devastation to the river's bridges, the one at Warcop withstood the full fury of the Eden. Today it stands, a magnificent, beautiful structure that is a credit to the village.

Brough Hill Fair, one of the oldest fairs in England, was established by Charter granted by Edward III to Robert de Clifford in 1329. Originally held at Brough Intack, it was moved to Brough Hill, about a mile west of the village, *circa* 1661 because of plague at Brough Intack. It was held on the two days preceding the feast of St. Matthew, September 21st, the day of the festival and the following day. At some unspecified date it became a two-day event, being held on September 30th and October 1st. Today it lasts only one day, September 30th.

Since 1942, when the site became the property of the War Department, trading has occupied a smaller area. Today there are fewer horses to trade and the gypsies who still gather there do so mainly to be reunited with members of their families and friends they have not seen for twelve months. On the other hand there are more gorgios who come by the bus-load to "gawp" and have their fortunes told.

* * *

The Eden Valley line had been planned to run from Warcop to

Brough before climbing steeply over Stainmore; but local farmers refused to sell land for that purpose and the Railway Company re-routed the line via Musgrave and Kirkby Stephen, where land was available. So Brough lost out. Not only did it lose a railway station, an engine shed and other railway-associated means of employment to Kirkby Stephen: the coming of the railway to the Eden Valley destroyed its coaching trade.

Situated between Brough and Warcop are the two villages of Great and Little Musgrave, which were separate townships until 1894 when they were united to form one parish called Musgrave. After the Norman Conquest the Manor of Musgrave was held by the family of the same name and most authorities, including Nicholson and Burn, consider that the place-name is derived from that family. *Burke's Peerage* suggests that, as is so often the case, the place gave the family their name. It is a matter for conjecture, but I think that *Burke's Peerage* is correct because the word means "mouse infested wood," a description that would relate better to a place than a family.

The first Musgrave known to have been associated with the place was called Peter. He lived there during King Stephen's reign. Thereafter the Musgraves held the manors of Great and Little Musgrave, nearby Soulby and others until just before the First World War.

The Musgraves lived at Great Musgrave until about 1350 when Thomas de Musgrave purchased Hartley, then called Harcla Castle, crenellated the buildings, added a stone tower and moved in. Although Hartley Castle is not many miles from Great Musgrave, once Thomas de Musgrave had moved there he appears to have simply abandoned his old home.

All that remains of the old feudal hall at Great Musgrave is an almost square mound with traces of what was once an outer wall surrounding it, enclosing an area of about 1.5 acres. This is to be found in a 2.5 acre field at the west end of Hall Garth.

The Musgraves lived at Hartley Castle, their only home, until the end of the reign of Henry VI, when Sir Thomas Musgrave married the heiress of Stapleton, who brought Edenhall into the family. From then until early in the 18th century they divided their time between the two residences.

About 1600 Sir Richard Musgrave added wings to Hartley Castle, enlarging it and transforming it into a mansion. Further additions were made in 1650, turning it into "a stately home and seat." It was demolished in the first quarter of the 18th century by Sir Christopher Musgrave, who removed the materials to repair Edenhall.

Edenhall has been demolished and the Musgraves are gone.

Great Musgrave straddles a hilltop commanding fine views over open country and the Eden. Its church, dedicated to St. Theobald, sits in a hollow beside the river. It was built in 1845-6 to replace one even closer to the river which, when there were floods, was flooded pew-deep. A path leads down from the village to the church, which can also be reached from the Kirkby Stephen road along an avenue of chestnut trees. Like St. Columba's, Warcop, St. Theobald's celebrates rushbearing every year on the first Sunday in July.

Little Musgrave lies across the river from its larger neighbour, on lower ground. It is a no-nonsense, no frills village, very much involved with farming, rather isolated and with no pub.

Scandal Beck, a major tributary of the upper Eden, is born some eight miles, as the crow flies, south of Soulby on the western flank of Little Fell. For the first few miles of its life it flows north-westerly to Ravenstonedale, gaining strength along the way from several feeders. Gradually it changes direction, heading N.N.E. as it enters the very picturesque Smardale ghyll.

This is an area of ancient settlements; and tumuli, known locally as Giants' Graves, are on both sides of the ghyll.

The Settle-Carlisle line crosses the northern or downstream end of Smardale ghyll on one of the largest stone-built viaducts in the country. Just over 700 feet long, it has twelve arches, each 45 feet high and crosses Scandal Beck at a height of 130 feet. The well known engineer Crossley designed it; building started in 1870 and it was completed in 1875. More than 60,000 tons of stone were used and the foundations had to be sunk some forty feet through clay until firm red shale was reached.

At Soulby the beck makes another change of direction to flow eastwards for a mile to its confluence with the Eden near Beckfoot. Two twisting miles downstream of this meeting of the waters and close to Great Musgrave Swindale Beck joins the Eden from the east. Midway between these two unions, and also from the east, the rivers Eden and Belah coalesce.

About the same length as Scandal Beck, the River Belah stems from several sikes draining the soft marches of Winton Fell to the east; an empty landscape.

Before the railway line from Kirkby Stephen to Darlington was axed the Belah was spanned by a magnificent iron viaduct, 1,000 feet long, 200 feet high and with a 60 feet span. There were 16 pillars and two stone buttresses. Mr Bouch, the engineer who later designed the Tay Bridge, designed Belah viaduct. It was built in 1859 and by any standards was a superb engineering feat. Amazingly it was built in only forty-three days. A document placed in the centre column of the eighth pier gave details of the construction in verse:

> To future ages these lines will tell
> Who built this structure o'er the dell -
> Wilson with these eighty men
> Raised Belah's viaduct o'er the glen.

Following the closure of the line the viaduct, a landmark for miles around, was demolished.

The middle reach of the Belah is along a particularly fine, wooded ghyll, close to the bottom of which a lovely old bridge crosses the river. It was built by a Stainmore man called Cuthbert Buckle who became Lord Mayor of London in 1593.

* * *

Margaret Hastwell was a Winton lass who went into service at Deepgill, hard by Little Fell, in Mallerstang. While there she courted and married James Faraday (1761-1810) who was a blacksmith at Outhgill. They had two children before moving to London, where their third child, Michael, was born. Michael (1791-1867), who was largely self-taught, was a brilliant scientist and great experimenter who discovered electromagnetic induction, the basis of electric power generation. His studies of electrolysis in the early 1830s laid the foundations of electro chemistry. The irony is that electricity, which resulted from Michael's experiments, did not reach Mallerstang, his father's birthplace, until September 1963!

On a stone above one of the windows of one of Winton's oldest houses is the following inscription: "R. and B.E. 1681. To all the dwelers in this place, God grant peace hapines and grace." This is Burn's House where one of the village's famous sons was born, *circa* 1720. Richard Burn, L.L.D., was vicar of Orton for forty years and became Chancellor of the Diocese of Carlisle. He wrote several books but is best remembered for his *History of the Antiquities of Cumberland and Westmorland,* which he wrote in conjunction with Joseph Nicholson. It is a standard work now much sought after by collectors. He died in 1785.

Winton Hall, with its mullioned, iron bar fronted windows and thick buttressed walls, is perhaps the oldest house in the village. It was the seat of the Scaife family. In 1664 Robert Scaife and his brother, Arthur, who lived at Helbeck Hall, were very much involved in building Winton's first primary school. One of the first governors of Appleby Grammar School was a member of the Scaife family of Winton. All in all, the Scaife family were early pioneers of education.

Winton's Manor House, a three-storied building, built in the Elizabethan-style, was formerly a boy's school run on similar lines to the one at Bowes on which Charles Dickens based "Dotheboys Hall" when he wrote *Nicholas Nickleby.* Following the public outcry caused by the book, neither Bowes nor Winton schools survived.

The back road from Winton to Kirkby Stephen passes Eden Place, a manor-house set back from it behind tall beech trees. Huge bird boxes have been attached to some of these trees, put there by the present owners to house their parrots. The birds are in no way restricted and are often to be seen in and around Kirkby Stephen.

Between Great Musgrave and Kirkby Stephen the river is crossed three times: first just beyond defunct Musgrave station, now a private dwelling, then at Blands Wath Farm and finally just beyond Winton Field Farm.

The Cloisters at Kirkby Stephen

10: Kirkby Stephen to Black Fell Moss via the Roman Road

Length of section:	11 miles
Total distance:	77 miles
Map:	O.S. Landranger 91 and 98
Handy Hostelry:	The Moorcock Inn.

Route Directions

From the eastern side of Kirkby Stephen market-place go down the alley between shops, turn right at the end of it, then left, down steps and continue straight ahead to Frank's Bridge, which cross. Turn right, upstream and at a kissing gate, where paths bifurcate take the right-hand, green one, along the river bank. Cross a tributary and go along a lane edging a wood. Keep along it past the wood and take the right-hand lane at a T junction which will bring you back to the river, which cross on a footbridge.

Turn left and go upstream close to the river on your left, first through fields, then through Stenkrith Park along a well defined path. Where it exits onto a road turn left, crossing the road diagonally and, before the bridge over the river is reached go through a stile on your right, down a flight of steps and right along a path, passing the remains of a railway bridge. Immediately beyond the bridge buttress go over the stile on your right into the pasture and follow the river bank upstream.

Where a wooded river bank looms ahead bear right and, keeping the wood on your left, go upstream, moving diagonally to the right to a gate in the field's top right-hand corner. Go through the gate and left, past a cottage, Halfpenny Gate, and along a concrete farm road to Wharton Hall. Passing the impressive gatehouse on your left continue along the concrete farm road until a bridge is reached over the river. Do not cross this bridge. Instead continue upstream through fields to enter a field containing a track from Wharton, seen on the right.

Turn left along the track and go along it to where, south of Birkett Common, it joins a tarmac road. Go downhill along the road to where

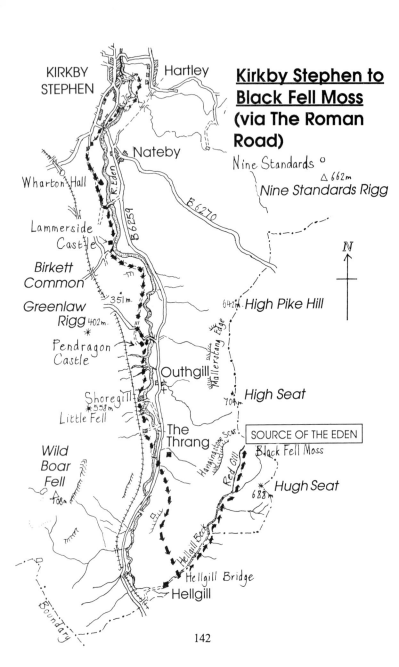

Kirkby Stephen to Black Fell Moss (via The Roman Road)

KIRKBY STEPHEN

Hartley

Nateby

Wharton Hall

Lammerside Castle

Birkett Common

Greenlaw Rigg 402m.

Pendragon Castle

351m.

Wild Boar Fell

708m

Shoregill *558m*

Little Fell

Outhgill

The Thrang

Nine Standards °

△ 662m

Nine Standards Rigg

N

High Pike Hill 642m

Mallerstang Edge

High Seat 709m

SOURCE OF THE EDEN

Black Fell Moss

Hugh Seat 688m

Red Gill

Hanginstone Scar

Hellgill Beck

Hellgill Bridge

Hellgill

Boundary

R. Eden

B6259

B6270

it bridges the river but do not cross. Turn right, instead, through a stile, and follow the river bank along a right of way, in parts clearly defined, in others not visible, passing Shoregill Farm.

Do not cross the bridge just upstream of Shoregill. Continue along a clear path by the riverside and along the field beyond it to where another bridge crosses the river. Again do not cross. Turn right, along a farm road to farm buildings, go between them and on, upstream, for a short distance to a fine pack-horse bridge. Cross this and climb the steep bank to the B6259, which cross. The large house to your left is The Thrang.

Go through a gate into a rough pasture with many rushes. The way is diagonally to the right climbing steadily. As the very rutted way climbs it becomes clearer to follow and the way ahead is clearly seen. After two miles, cross Hell Gill Bridge and immediately turn left, climbing over the brow of a hill. Continue upstream with Hell Gill on your left and continue, climbing stiles over "Eurofence" where necessary. Follow the main stream, ignoring any feeders, all of which are not as wide as the main stream, and after about two miles slightly north-west of Hugh Seat, on Black Fell Moss the source of the Eden is reached.

The Background Story

The house in which I was born occupied one end of a terrace of four, built on the site of a mill on the inside of a bend in the river. My first clear recollections of Kirkby Stephen, then, were of those stone dwellings, the river flowing past them and Mrs Charlton's ducks.

Each day, when she let them out, they would waddle, Indian file, to the river. There, except in times of flood they would spend long hours foraging, preening and sleeping, their heads tucked behind them into their backs. Often they would swim upstream, exploring the shallows. The waterfall in front of the houses presented no problems. They would swim close to it, then, if fancy took them, leave the water, shuffle over the stones and into the coarse grasses and rushes between the fall and the remains of the weir. Then, having selected suitable spots, one or two of them would lay eggs: and jolly good they tasted, too!

The ducks would enter the water at a ford slightly upstream of narrow, 17th century, double-arched Frank's Bridge, leading from the town side of the river, its left bank, into a large pasture called the Hills Bottom. This quaint span has gained a certain repute as a model for landscape painters.

Not to be outdone by a mere footbridge, Hills Bottom itself seeks an even greater glory. Not only does it house the town's cricket and hockey pitches, not only did the now defunct local football team, Kirkby Stephen Harriers, use it for home matches, but the surrounding hill slopes that turned the field into a natural amphitheatre, were ideally suited for sledging. Sadly this is no longer the case because great chunks of what were once open pasture have been fenced off. Yet, Just before World War II the whole of this magnificent field, which is so eminently suited to leisure activities, was offered to the Parish Council at the peppercorn cost of £100 by the then owner, Mr Cleasby of Hartley Fold: unbelievably, the offer was turned down.

The Temperance Movement, which, by the middle of the 19th century had become well established in the Eden Valley, held its first Vale of Eden, Band of Hope union demonstration in 1873. Since then this has been an annual event, alternating, except on rare occasions, between Appleby and Kirkby Stephen, the venue at the latter being the Hills Bottom.

Until 1954, when the day was changed to a Saturday, every demonstration was held on a Thursday. Taylor's Roundabouts, who wintered in the Carlisle area and toured during the summer months, always arrived on the Hills Bottom during the early part of that week, set up for business ready for *the* day and moved away on the following Sunday.

It was the coming and going that caused most problems, not the building up and pulling down. This was because the only way in and out of the field for the big stuff, the steam engines, the huge diesel trucks, the living wagons and the heavily laden packing trucks, was across the ford just upstream of Frank's Bridge.

To reach the ford all the vehicles had to descend a steep hill and squeeze obliquely between the end house of a small terrace and a large, oddly shaped building that, in its time, had been a brewery, a creamery and, during World War II, Home Guard H.Q.. Easing through the narrow gap was slow, arduous work, for there was little room to manoeuvre; and when each vehicle was clear there was still the river to cross.

This operation never failed to attract a large number of interested onlookers. They crowded along Frank's Bridge and spilled into the Hills Bottom, frequently getting dangerously close to the wire hawsers, the better to see how the showmen tackled the crossing.

Fairs and markets of a different kind - cattle and sheep - have played an important part in Kirkby Stephen life since Edward III granted a charter to Roger de Clifford, Baron of Westmorland, for two yearly fairs to be held there on St. Mark's and St. Luke's days and the day following and a market every Friday. James I, by his charter in 1606, changed it to one market on a Monday and two fairs yearly, one on the Wednesday, Thursday and Friday after Whitsuntide and the other on the two days before St. Luke's day and on the day itself.

The Monday market is still held. The Whitsuntide fair is obsolete. St. Luke's Fair is still held every October. At one time trade in cattle and sheep was particularly brisk. The cattle occupied the market square and all the available space along North Road. The sheep were in pens which extended from in front of the King's Arms Hotel, along Market Street, around Sow Pow - now Victoria Square - and so far along Mellbecks. There is a round flag in Market Street known as the charter stone and it was from there that a magistrate or other prominent citizen read the charter. Luke's Fair, always an important means of enabling farmers to dispose of their surplus stock, was a great meeting place, especially for sheep farmers from the dales. Now it has been superseded by the auction mart, which my great grandfather and two associates established and is now owned by Kidds of Penrith.

Kirkby Stephen is very much older than its fairs. Man was living in the area during the Stone Age, 7,000 to 5,000BC, and Bronze Age earthworks and burial mounds give evidence of pre-Roman settlements thereabouts. The name Kirkby is derived from the Norse words *Kirke* and *Bye*, meaning church town. Stephen is a little more obscure. The parish church, which is dedicated to St. Stephen, was given by Ivo Taillebois to St. Mary's York, of which Stephen was an abbot. Maybe the affix refers to him.

After Kendal, the parish church, the "Cathedral of the Dales," is the largest in what was Westmorland. There was probably a Saxon building on the site of the present church in the 8th century, which was destroyed by the Danes. Just inside the main entrance to the church there is an 11th century cross depicting Loki, the bound devil of the Norse invaders.

The church contains two chapels, one belonging to the Musgraves of Hartley Castle, the other to the Whartons of Wharton Hall. In the Hartley chapel are the resting places of three members of the Musgrave family who took over the occupancy of nearby Hartley Castle when Andrew de Harcla incurred royal displeasure and forfeited his life. A slab of red sandstone inside the altar space is believed to commemorate Sir Thomas de Musgrave who died about 1376. In the N.W. angle of the chapel an altar tomb is assigned to Sir Richard de Musgrave (1442). When the tomb was removed about 1847 a boar's tusk was found, thus supporting the legend that Sir Richard killed the last wild boar on nearby Wild Boar Fell. The tomb of his grandson, Sir Richard Kt. (d.1464) and his wife bears the Arms of the family.

The Wharton chantry contains an elaborate altar tomb carrying three full length figures, Thomas, first Lord Wharton, with his first wife on his right and his second on his left. It is a replica of the first Lord Wharton's real tomb which is in Healaugh church, near Tadcaster. He founded Kirkby Stephen Grammar School in 1566. The baronetcy was conferred on Thomas for inflicting a severe defeat on the Scottish army at Solway Moss in 1542. His son witnessed the Will of Queen Mary and is buried in Westminster Abbey. The third Lord received James I at Wharton Hall in 1617; and it was his son, "the good Lord Wharton" who founded a bible trust which still operates. The good Lord's son attained the rank of Marquess and was a leading Whig. His son became a duke while still a minor, but he squandered the family fortune, supported the Jacobite cause, and died on a bed of straw in Spain. The Wharton estates were then confiscated, much going to the Lowthers. The title was not revived until 1916 and the last holder of it died in 1969 and it is again in abeyance.

Once, about 150 years ago, there were seventeen public houses in Kirkby Stephen: now there are five and the town is unique in having more places of worship (six) than pubs.

The oldest Youth Hostel in Westmorland and one of the oldest in the country was opened in Kirkby Stephen above the Friends' Meeting House in 1931. In 1981 it was moved to more spacious premises in the former Methodist chapel on Fletcher Hill.

From Fletcher Hill, looking north, St. Stephen's lovely church tower dominates the scene. Closer inspection entails a pleasant walk along broad Market Street to the market square, which from Fletcher Hill is hidden behind a block of buildings. From the market square, with its war memorial and memories of bull baiting days, the main entrance to the church is through the cloisters, which for a long time were used as a butter market on market days. They were built in 1810 to the wish of a naval officer and until World War II were enclosed by iron railings. Well looked after these days they add charm and character to the town.

In the churchyard, just through the cloisters, there is a large, flat tomb reputed to belong to the Whartons. Known as the Truppstone, it was there that money in lieu of farm produce was paid to the incumbent of the church on Easter Monday. This ancient custom ended in 1836 when all tithes were commuted by the Tithes Commutation Act.

There is an interesting old building opposite the market square known as the Shambles, which has a long spinning gallery in the upper storey.

Either of the two passages, Walton's Yard or Stoneshot, leading from the market square or the Little Wiend, near Martin's Bank, will bring you to Frank's Bridge.

The Eden approaches Kirkby Stephen in a most spectacular way, squeezing through a narrow gorge overhung with birch and rowan, then fanning across a pink, brockram bedrock fissured and pockmarked by countless floods, to plunge beneath a high bridge carrying the Kirkby Stephen to Nateby road into a hole so wide it reaches both sides of the river and so plagued by dangerous undercurrents it is unsafe to swim there even when the river is low. This fantastic pot hole - in the vernacular "cow carny hole," - is terrifying in times of flood and the swollen river thundering into it can be heard from afar, for all the world like the roar of an express train. Downstream of the bridge, the river pours in a most picturesque way through Stenkrith Wood, sluicing along channels worn in the brockram, swilling over shallow falls and swirling in the pot holes, twirling the loose pebbles contained therein.

Where the fall ends in a large, deep pool, edged with tall trees, Black Dub, the brockram gives way to sandstone; not by degrees but clearly, as though cut with a knife. Black Dub marks the uppermost end of the sandstone the Eden has flowed across all the way to the Solway Firth.

On both sides of the river as it leaves the five miles long valley of Mallerstang there is much evidence of old patterns of cultivation. In several pastures long strip lynchets run across the hillside, through and beyond the dry stone walls which enclosed the field at a much later date. The most striking examples can be seen from the Kirkby Stephen to Sedbergh road where the terraces sweep over Gallows Hill near Wharton Hall.

Wharton Hall, "farmstead on an embankment," was the place to which the de Quertons moved from nearby Lammerside Castle in the 14th century. Lammerside Castle, "Lambert's shieling," a 14th century peel tower, was the original home of the Whartons and all that remains of it today is the ground floor which is divided into five compartments with barrel vaulting overhead. Wharton Hall, which occupies a grand site at the top of a high bank on a bend of the river, was once surrounded by a large deer park. It is built around a courtyard and has been enlarged from time to time. In 1540 Thomas, Lord Wharton, added a new great hall with a large kitchen. The gatehouse was added in 1559 and there are traces of the shaft for the portcullis still to be seen. Above the entrance which leads through an archway into the courtyard there is a tablet carved with the Wharton Arms and the motto *"Pleasur in acts darmys,"* also dated 1559.

Wharton Hall is in the parish of Nateby, out of sight of Nateby village, which straddles the side of a spur of the Pennines on the other side of the river. If you take the left-hand fork from the village and follow the road that climbs steeply up Tailbridge it will take you over Birkdale Common to Keld at the top end of Swaledale. But if you go straight through the village the scenic, undulating winding road will take you through the narrow vale of Mallerstang to the 9.5 miles distant Moorcock Inn.

Mallerstang is a narrow valley five miles long soaring to over two thousand feet on either side. Railway, river and road all run through it, parallel to each other. Farmsteads are scattered along the vale bottom in splendid isolation, the only group of dwellings being the hamlet of Outhgill, mid-way along it.

Mallerstang Edge spreads along most of the eastern side of the valley. It rises to a height of 2,257 feet at Hugh's Seat where Lady

Anne Clifford had a pillar built as a boundary mark in 1664. Several becks draining this spongy fellside flow westwards over the rim of the escarpment in a series of spectacular milk churns of foaming, tumbling water. But sometimes, when these young streams meet the full force of a westerly wind head on, the effort is all too much and the water is flung back on itself as a fine spray. When seen from the valley floor, it looks for all the world like smoke being pulled from the chimney of a hidden house. When seen from close quarters on the Edge itself the effect is equally dramatic and much wetter.

The western side of the valley is dominated by Wild Boar Fell at its southern end. Because Wild Boar Fell with its Neb and spectacular Scriddles looks the part and maybe because its height, 2,324 feet, is easy to remember, it is often regarded as Mallerstang's real mountain. Perhaps it is; but the summit of High Seat on Mallerstang Edge is four feet higher!

When the Vikings settled in north-west England they called the wild uplands which so much reminded them of their homeland, *fiall,* which in the old Norse means mountain. Fell is a variant of that name and has more to do with character than elevation.

The fells which are the Eden Valley's eastern boundary throughout its length and include Cross Fell, the highest ground in England's backbone, were given the name Pennine by Charles Bertram during the 18th century. The name Pennines - *penn* meaning hill - accurately describes this hill system but Pennine Chain is a misnomer because the hills do not form an unbroken line.

Wild Boar Fell is magnificent. It dominates the dale and is a landmark for miles around. Often with its head in the clouds, it lifts its rocky face from a limestone plateau which is pitted with deep, dangerous holes. On clear days the views from its summit are panoramic. But in stormy weather when howling winds scream across its rain-lashed head the mountain is fearful. Under such conditions it is a place to be avoided.

Wild Boar Fell is a refuge for many creatures including ravens and foxes. On one occasion, while on a ledge just below the Nab I chanced to look down and saw, below me, and unaware of my presence, an adult fox in prime condition moving purposefully along the foot of the escarpment. It was a privileged peep into the wonderful world of Nature and one that remains with me still, locked in memory.

During the Roman occupation Mallerstang forest spread far beyond the confines of the vale, merged with Stainmore and Inglewood forests, and ended only when the site of the as yet unbuilt Carlisle was reached. The whole length and breadth of the Eden Valley was a boundless forest of oak, ash, birch and alder undergrown with tangled thorns. Sunlight was unable to penetrate these dense woods and reach the soaking morasses underfoot. Roman slaves, the native Britons, constructed paved causeways through the swamps: otherwise they were left to the wild boar, wild cat, wild deer and wild bulls.

Now most of the woods have gone and many of the morasses have been drained and turned into good agricultural land. The ghylls are still tree-lined and Jenny Wood, with its falls, remains to enchant. But it is mostly dry stone walls, not hedges, that divide the fields.

In springtime primroses, celandines and anemones, those sweet harbingers of summer, bring colour and promise of warmer days. Then come the bluebells and after them, when the days are at their longest, the mellifluous summer flowers. On those days when summer sunshine fills the vale with hazy laziness and the sweet smell of new mown hay hangs heavy on the still air many visitors, fooled by the languid aspects it presents drool and sigh and express the desire to live in such an idyllic spot. They forget, if, indeed, they ever knew, that such days are rare in Mallerstang.

Those who live in the dale all the year round get more than their fair share of foul weather. Winter after winter, with few exceptions, the whole valley finds itself cut off from the outside world by deep drifts. Many are over twenty feet deep; and snow takes some shifting. Then there is the cold. Icy winter winds often blow for weeks and can match the Helm for frigidity. When the thaw begins the Eden, swollen with snow broth, becomes an angry torrent, uprooting trees, sweeping away cattle and poultry and flooding low-lying areas like Water Gate Bottom.

Then there are the violent thunderstorms which develop around Wild Boar and neighbouring fells at the tail end of a period of oppressive weather. The rain released is so powerful, so heavy and so concentrated, the volume so great that the released water hurls itself along with great violence as a downstream flowing bore, sweeping away anything vulnerable in its path. One famous one on Stainmore swept across a road with such force, when the culvert was unable to contain the water, that it washed away a large part of it. Other thunderstorms of even greater violence and destructive force have had their origins on the Mallerstang fells. On several occasions I, along with other locals, have helped the police in their grim task of finding the bodies of young children tragically swept away as a consequence of a "pash."

"Watter Yat Bottom," which is "Water Gate Bottom" in Westmorland vernacular, is a small plain, very popular with family picnickers, which spreads across the lower end of Mallerstang. Every autumn fell ponies and their foals are rounded up and herded there before being sold at a nearby farm. This sale takes the place of the annual Cowper Day sales which used to be held in Kirkby Stephen.

There are about forty burial barrows of various kinds within a fifteen mile radius of Kirkby Stephen. Neolithic mounds called Long Barrows are the oldest. Then come the New Bronze Age Round Barrows and lastly smaller tumuli averaging 20 feet by 10 feet. There are two of these smaller ones close to the left bank of the river on Birkett Common. They present a puzzle because most tumuli are on high ground where the early men who built them lived. Why would these two be built on ground that in those days would have been marshy and covered in woodland?

Where the dale begins to spread over Watter Yat Bottom there is a farm called Dale Foot. In Lady Anne's day it was called Blue Grass and Noncomformist Captain Robert Atkinson lived there. During the Civil War he commanded a troop of horse and for a time was Governor of Appleby Castle. A braggart and self-seeker who was completely disloyal to his friends, Atkinson had a very brutal side to his nature. One Sunday afternoon in September, 1648, he killed Richard Darby of Kirkby Stephen in a field near Pendragon Castle. Two years later he led Lady Anne's tenants when they asked for a re-assessment of their rents. After the Restoration he became a spy for Sir Philip Musgrave, the leading Royalist in the district. Yet his Nonconformist friends still trusted him. His involvement in the Kaber Rigg Plot was his downfall. He had become a double agent for his own ends. In Sir Philip Musgrave's eyes the man was a traitor and deserved to die. Because of his activities during the Commonwealth, Lady Anne's attitude towards him was equally cold. And while waiting for his fate to be made known his attitude throughout his

Pendragon Castle

time as a prisoner at Carlisle was insolent. Yet despite all this, a warrant to reprieve him was issued to the High Sheriff of Durham on August 31st, 1664, following a visit by two assize judges to Appleby on 20th of that month. September 1st had been set as execution day. The reprieve was wrongly directed and did not reach Appleby until after Atkinson's death. Perhaps it was poetic justice.

His widow continued to live at Blue Grass until her death in 1667. His descendants continued to live there until 1925.

The origin of Pendragon Castle goes back into dimmest antiquity to an age dominated by fiction and the element of mystery. When the Bottom of Westmorland was part of Northumbria, one of the seven kingdoms, Uther was one of those kings, the word being an abbreviation of Ughtred, a personal name. Pendragon was a descriptive title, conferred by the Saxons on the head of an army, like commander-in-chief is today. *Pen* in Saxon usage is head or chief and *dragon* is warrior. There may be doubts about Uther Pendragon's lifestyle but there is no doubt at all about his etymology. His occupation as commander-in-chief of an army is established.

The castle itself was built about the sixth century at a time when

English history was at its most turbulent. Everybody was having a go at everybody else: local tribes fought each other, then joined forces to fight invading Saxons, then stood side by side with the Saxons against the barbaric Picts who had broken through Hadrian's Wall and were bloodstaining northern England. Uther found he had plenty of work to do.

The original Pendragon Castle was a wooden structure: the age of building stout, stone castles arrived with the Normans some 500 years later. Tradition credits Uther with having built Stonehenge, yet he was unable to ring Pendragon with a moat:

> "Let Uther Pendragon do what he can,
> The Eden will run where the Eden ran."

The couplet tells the story, one of many about the father of the famous King Arthur.

When Sir Hugh de Morville, a later occupant of Pendragon, looked out of a south-facing window in the castle keep on his return home from murdering Thomas Becket, Archbishop of Canterbury, that December day in 1170, it put the fear of God into him. It is a magnificent view, with Wild Boar Fell prominent in it. But what caught de Morville's eye and held him spellbound was the dead Archbishop lying across his vision, his mitre on his head. Now, Sir Hugh had not actually struck the man of God. His part in the murder had been to ward off anyone trying to interfere "so that the others might with greater freedom licence perpetuate the crime." But he was as guilty as they were; and seeing the dead Becket lying there he took it as a sign of ill-boding. He was right. Henry II suspended him from his office as Justice for the counties of Northumberland and Cumberland and confiscated his estates. What de Morville saw was real enough. I have seen it many times as you can if you stand in the right spot and look in the right direction.

King John restored the estate to Robert de Veteripont, whose mother, Maud, was Huge de Morville's sister. These were divided, in 1268, between Idonea de Leybourne and Isabelle de Clifford and from then on remained in the hands of the Clifford family. Idonea inherited both Pendragon and Brough castles; but her favourite was Pendragon where she died in 1334.

Edward Balliol, former King of the Scots, was entertained at

Pendragon Castle by Roger de Clifford in 1337. Four years later more Scots visited it in greater numbers while Edward I was getting himself involved in the Hundred Years War. They were border raiders and attacked the castle, burning what they could of it and leaving it ruinous. Roger de Clifford restored it about 1360-70. Two hundred years later the Scots again set it on fire and it remained in ruins until that redoubtable Lady Anne Clifford repaired it in 1660.

She re-roofed the keep, built battlement walls twelve feet thick, two gates, stables, a coach house, brew house, wash house and a little chamber over "the gate that is arched." She also built the nearby lovely bridge over the Eden. It was a magnificent castle again.

After her death it was dismantled by the sixth Earl of Thanet to whom her estates had passed. Much of what remained collapsed in 1773 and the structure continue to decay until the remains were taken over by the Ministry of Works.

A lot more restoration work could be done to this ancient pile which holds so much of our history in its mellow stones. Perhaps English Heritage will emulate Lady Anne Clifford and develop it, thus giving back to it some of its former splendour. For despite its knocked about appearance Pendragon Castle is precious because it binds us to our roots and gives us pride in our rich heritage.

It took six years to build the Settle-Carlisle line which runs through Mallerstang: six years of punishing unrelenting toil to forge a splendid railway across some of the wildest country in England. It was a line the Midland was reluctant to build and one that, 113 years later, the people refused to allow to die. It was opened in August, 1875, for goods traffic when there was only one track through Mallerstang, and for passenger traffic on May 1st, the following year.

Often working in atrocious weather, the navvies, mostly Irish and Welsh, lived in hutted camps erected at intervals along the line. There were two camps in Mallerstang: on Aisgill Moor and on Birkett Fell. They were cheerless places in which, far from the restraining influences of home and family, the men spent most of their spare time drinking heavily. This frequently led to fights and sometimes to pitched battles between rival gangs.

There is a signal box at Aisgill summit, 1,169 feet above sea level and the highest point on the line. There is another, Mallerstang box, lower down the dale. Both boxes played a prominent roll in the serious crash of September 1913 when due to human error, a night express from Carlisle ran into the back of another, killing 16 passengers. The crash occurred half a mile short of Aisgill summit.

* * *

Apart from some work on the railway, the sole occupation in Mallerstang is sheep farming and milk production. In the low-lying valley bottom there are meadows and pastures with enclosed rough grazing above them and, higher still, the open fell with its unlimited stray.

In the 10th and 11th centuries all Mallerstang was unfenced and undivided except by boundary stones. By the 12th century the population throughout England was beginning to increase appreciably. This led, by the 16th century, to more attention being given to sheep. Better breeds were introduced so that the momentum of the wool trade might be maintained. In many parts of the country arable land was converted to pasture. Mallerstang had no arable land so it turned its attention to the lower slopes of the fells and they were enclose with dry stone walls. Most of this work was done in the late 18th century. This work also had the advantage of clearing the land of loose stones. There was no set pattern for these walls, which were built mostly by lead miners from Keld, who found that a good living could be made in walling by contract, being paid by the rood.

At lambing time these boundary walls provided shelter for the sheep; and they climbed high, these walls, some to under the shadow of Wild Boar Fell itself. Most are almost 200 years old and still stand up to the very worst of Cumbrian winters. Any gaps that appear are quickly repaired by the local farmers.

At about the beginning of the 18th century the sheep in Mallerstang were either native or a cross with Scotch lambs. There was no attempt, at that time, to improve either the carcass or the fleece.

By 1823 the local cattle had been supplanted by the shorthorns which were beginning to become popular by 1837.

The development of pure breeds of sheep was one of the most remarkable features of agricultural progress in the 19th century. For during that time Swaledale, rough fell and Scotch black-faced sheep had developed from the black-faced heath breed which had been the chief breed in 1842.

About 1960 the cattle were northern dairy shorthorns, non-pedigree shorthorns and Friesian Cross with some Aberdeen-Angus for beef. Today Friesians predominate.

Today's sheep are Swaledales, a very hardy breed, well able to withstand bad weather and to thrive on poor pastures. Most flocks are permanent and go with the farm so that when a farm is sold the purchaser buys the sheep also. The flocks on the open fell keep to their own grazing or heath and know what part to graze at different seasons and where shelter can be found in bad weather.

Mallerstang farmers work by the weather and at the first sign of snow they bring the sheep down from the fells. Sometimes, however, the weather beats them as in the disastrous winter of 1947 when a great many sheep died. Yet so hardy are the Swaledales that they have been known to survive being buried under snow for three weeks.

Mallerstang had probably the worst experience of all Westmorland in the 1947 snow storm, the worst in living memory. Every house was cut off for several weeks, fuel supplies became dangerously low and many households ran out of domestic supplies. Farmers were unable to obtain feeding stuffs and even water became difficult to obtain. A ton of hay loaned by farmer W.J. Dent of Kaber Fold, north of Kirkby Stephen was loaded onto a railway wagon at Kirkby Stephen West Station and taken to a point near Mallerstang signal box. There it was tipped over an embankment and delivered to various farms by sledge. The same method was used to deliver food from Kirkby Stephen shopkeepers. If anything, the winter of 1963 "hap-up" was even worse. More snow fell than in 1947 and the winds were savage. Ten times blizzards closed the road to Outhgill and ten times it was cleared by men from the County Council Highways Department. The Eden, close to Dale Foot, flowed under a vast snowdrift. Workmen a little further upstream had to clear cuttings 25 feet deep and, in Outhgill many houses were snowed up to bedroom window height.

Bishop Rainbow, in his sermon at Lady Anne's funeral, spoke of her habit of travelling by "mountainous and almost impossible ways, that she might make the poor people and labourers her pioneers, who were always rewarded for their pains." One such road, which she used when travelling between Skipton and Pendragon Castle was an ancient track, thought to have been built by the Romans. It starts in the hamlet of Wharton, on the valley slopes west of Birkdale Common and its way is by Lammerside Castle, Sandpot, Shoregill and Deepgill farms. It crosses the Eden at Thrang Bridge and goes diagonally up Mallerstang Fell to cross Hell Gill Bridge before gradually dropping down to Shaw Paddock and from there into Wensleydale. It is one of the finest walks in the district, giving splendid views of Wild Boar and others fells across the vale. The first mile of climb from Thrang Bridge is overgrown with rushes and deeply rutted but its direction is fairly clear. As it crosses level ground on top of the escarpment behind Ing Heads and Hanging Lund it becomes a clearly defined, close-cropped, green way, some 20 feet wide. This changes to mud as Hell Gill Bridge is approached.

For the greater part of any year there was little movement on the Roman road. In the 18th century strings of pack-horses used it bringing goods from Wensleydale to busy Kendal. Frequently they would act as carriers of woollen articles knitted during long winter evenings by the Mallerstang farm folk. But twice a year, at Brough Hill Fair time, when droves of Scotch cattle were sold there, and in spring, when local cattle were driven to the Yorkshire sales, the road

'Steam Special' in Mallerstang

was very "thrang" indeed. It was at these times that enterprising women, some from as far away as Ravenstonedale, would set up wayside stalls at places like Hell Gill Bridge and sell apples and gingerbread to the drovers. At other times the arrival of the pedlar at a lonely farm was an eagerly awaited event because, apart from his wares, he brought gossip and news of national events, albeit garbled.

Throughout its length the Roman road was seldom more than 8 feet wide, making travel along it difficult for wheeled vehicles. Furthermore, the steep inclines were not suitable for carriages.

In 1825, as part of an extension to an already existing turnpike road system, work began on a road which would keep to the valley bottom and join the Roman road at Shaw Paddock. It was to be a turnpike road, the toll bar being placed across the road just south of Castle Cottages, but wider and less exposed than the Roman road and without the latter's steep inclines.

It was opened on October 19th, 1829, and at once became a popular addition to the dale. The new road and the new railway line which came 47 years later marked the end of the old isolation in the dales.

Hell Gill is a fearsome rocky gorge, so narrow at its rim in places that, it is said anyone with a strong nerve can easily jump across it. Of course, if he doesn't quite make it, the chances are that he will not try again, for its average depth is 60 feet; deepening in some places to 90 feet. Far better to use the high-sided bridge, built about 1820 to replace an earlier pack-horse bridge.

Several highwaymen "worked" the ancient route from Wensleydale to the Eden Valley, including John "Swift Nick" Nevison, who sought its remoteness whenever the heat was on, and three locals, Ned Ward, Riddle and Broderick. One hard pressed hold-up man is said to have leaped Hell Gill from Westmorland into Yorkshire. In all probability it was Ned Ward, who was with Broderick at Shoregill when the latter was apprehended. Following an exciting chase up the valley, by Boggle Green and Hall Hill, he escaped.

The lively, infant Eden splashes over a great many beautiful waterfalls, the highest of which is spectacular Hell Gill Foss, about half a mile downstream of Hell Gill.

There are no trees above Hell Gill. Upstream of the gorge everything changes dramatically. The Eden that flows out of it pours in as Hell Gill Beck, which was not the name it was given at birth. The Eden begins life as Red Gill Beck. Its cradle is squelchy moorland, as wild and moody as the prevailing weather. Its first lusty gurples have as counterpoint the melodious cry of the curlew. To an exiled Westmerian it is the most evocative sound, pure liquid gold, a beautiful lamentation.

Noisily and swiftly and not yet a river it tumbles along its stony bed between high banks of spongy fell. Tiny sikes swell it, vainly trying to drain Black Fell Moss, which spreads across the 2,000 feet contour.

11: Kirkby Stephen to Black Fell Moss via Wild Boar Fell
(A longer more difficult alternative to Chapter 10)

Length of section:	15 miles
Total distance:	81 miles
Map:	O.S. Landranger 91 and 98
Handy hostelry:	The Moorcock Inn.

Route Directions

From Kirkby Stephen to Wharton Hall the route directions are as given in the previous chapter.

From Wharton Hall take the concrete farm road to Bullgill Farm where follow the green track between dry stone walls over the Settle-Carlisle line onto open fell. Continue in a S.S.W. direction, climbing steadily to cross an unfenced minor road after 0.75 of a mile. Keep going in a southerly direction across Wharton Fell, climbing steadily, to a wall bordering some heather allotments. Follow the wall to its end where climb steeply to the summit of Little Fell. The way continues southwards, gradually downwards at first then climbing steeply along the escarpment rim to the Nab. Keeping close to the escarpment top, continue for 0.5 of a mile to the next headland, identified by six cairns, where go N.W. for 0.5 of a mile to the summit (2,324ft.). Go south-west, inclining southwards, crossing a fence, using a stile, cross the depression between Wild Boar Fell and Swarth Fell. Join a wall coming up from Uldale and continue along Swarth Fell with the wall on your right to the two cairns on Swarth Fell Pike, where go left, downhill, across Ais Gill Moor to the cottages on the B6259. Go down the farm road to the right of the cottages, crossing the Settle-Carlisle line, and stay with it to the Roman road, just beyond Hellgill Farm, the way is now N.W., climbing steadily for 1.5 miles to easily recognised Hangingstone Scar, where, on a compass bearing, go due east for a mile to Red Gill on Black Fell Moss, the source of the Eden.

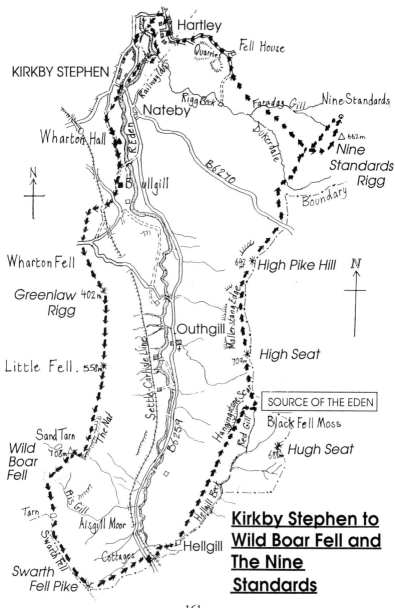

KIRKBY STEPHEN

Hartley

Fell House

Quarries

Railway Tarn

Rigg Beck

Nateby

R Eden

Wharton Hall

Faraday Gill

Nine Standards

Dukerdale

△ 662m

Nine
Standards
Rigg

Boundary

B6270

Bullgill

N

Wharton Fell

High Pike Hill

642m

N

Greenlaw 402m
Rigg

Mallerstang Edge

Settle-Carlisle Line

Outhgill

High Seat

709m

Little Fell. 558m

SOURCE OF THE EDEN

Black Fell Moss

The Nab

B6259

Sand Tarn

Hanging stone Scar

Red Gill

Hugh Seat

688m

Wild
Boar
Fell

708m

Ais Gill

Tarn

Alsgill Moor

Swarth Fell

Cottages

Hellgill

Hell gill Beck

Hellgill

**Kirkby Stephen to
Wild Boar Fell and
The Nine
Standards**

Swarth
Fell Pike

The Background Story

In 1982 Peter Denby, a member of the Kirkby Stephen Fell Search Team and Richard Sewell, a member of the Sedbergh Fell Rescue Team, together designed a circular walk beginning in Kirkby Stephen market-square. It was 23 miles long and took in some of the finest fell walking in the Upper Eden Valley. They called it the Mallerstang Horseshoe and Nine Standards Yomp. By happy chance it coincides, for the most part, with the airy, alternative final section of the Eden Valley Way, which also runs along the rim of Mallerstang's western escarpment. It is a good walk that gives a panoramic picture of Mallerstang, highlights the valley's glacial origins and illustrates how it fits into the surrounding countryside. It is well worth the energy expended on it; especially when fair Eden is preening herself in the sun, purring to the gentle motions of a soft breeze and Wild Boar Fell itself slices the contours of a broad, blue sky. For then you will see it at its best.

It is not as it was. Some 300,000 years ago Mallerstang was not a valley at all. It was a high plateau lying under a great glacier with just a few peaks thrusting through the thick ice. The same glacier covered the whole of northern Britain. The Ice Age was not continuous. It was divided into four periods separated by warm inter-glacial periods. When the great glacier began to push from the west over the Shap Fells, along the Eden Valley, over Stainmore and Mallerstang, that was when the great gouging began. Exerting tremendous pressures, the great glacier continued pushing eastward through parts of Durham and Yorkshire to spend itself beneath the shallow waters of the North Sea.

One of the tiny becks draining Wild Boar and Swarth Fells is thought by some geologists to have been the original source of the Eden. Ais Gill is its name and it drains part of Aisgill Moor. In their opinion Red Gill Beck, which has been the source of the Eden since before man populated Mallerstang, was originally a tributary of the River Ure, which flows eastwards. It rises near Hugh Seat, 2,257ft., on lonely, Black Fell Moss. Glacial movements and deposits, they claim, caused it to divert south-westwards, then northwards; and perhaps they are right. For the course of Hell Gill Beck runs parallel to the Ure for a mile, half a mile apart from it, separated by a watershed. But if the geologists are correct and Ais Gill was the original source, it held that distinction but briefly. For 300,000 years Black Fell Moss has been its cradle, firmly established by time. William Mounsey knew that in 1850 as we do today.

Ais Gill, meaning water gill, springs to life very close to the summit of Wild Boar Fell. It collects the waters from at least four sikes before emptying into the Eden below Aisgill Farm. On its journey down the escarpment it spills in a series of waterfalls through two ravines, White Kirk and Low White Kirk, which are well worth exploring for they are home to many interesting plants and mosses.

There is the feel of a real mountain about Wild Boar Fell. It sits on a deep bed of limestone, a great pile of sandstone and shale, capped with millstone grit. Once peat was cut on its western flanks, lime burned, stone quarried, lead mined and millstones fashioned. Today all these industries are silent and neglected. Now flocks of heafed sheep and free-range ponies share its broad plateau with foxes, ravens, curlews and discerning walkers.

Tradition has it that the last wild boar in Westmorland was killed on that lonely upland and gave it its name. A boar's tusk found in a walled grave in the Musgrave chapel in Kirkby Stephen parish church during restoration work in 1847 added credence to this belief.

The most spectacular route to the summit of Wild Boar Fell is up its steep escarpment, beginning where Ais Gill Beck pours under the B6259 near Aisgill Farm, eight miles south of Kirkby Stephen. The alternative Eden Valley Way route is an equally exciting, much longer way which coincides with the valley bottom route until about half a mile south of Wharton Hall.

When, after 500 years, Philip, the only son of Thomas, first Marquis of Wharton, the man who wrote the words to *Lilli Burlero*, fought against his country at the Siege of Gibraltar in 1727, and as a consequence was outlawed, deprived of all his titles and had his estates confiscated, that should have marked the end of the Wharton clan. But while Wharton Hall and the estates at Kirkby Stephen and Shap were purchased from the Crown by the Lowthers, many members of the Wharton clan emigrated to the New World where they spread and multiplied.

The original Wharton Hall was built during the 14th century and consisted of a hall with two cross wings. About 1540 a new great hall with a kitchen was added to the south-east of the original building and a few years later, in 1559, its impressive gatehouse was added. Today a rear wall, kitchen and huge fireplace are all that remain of the great hall. But Wharton Hall is occupied and the present owners have done a lot of restoration work on it. How good it is to know that this stately edifice and similar historic buildings are not only being preserved but are enhanced by loving ownership! The Chippendales have, in Wharton Hall, a working farm that has retained much of its original character. Thanks to their restoration work they have enhanced the quality of the area and made themselves a lovely home into the bargain. But then, they are lovely, caring people. The world could do with more of the same ilk.

A concrete farm road climbs from Wharton Hall to Bullgill, one of the farms making up the scattered hamlet of Wharton Dykes. It passes well above Lammerside Castle, the 14th century pele tower built to guard Mallerstang. The name is a corruption of Lambert's shieling and at one time it belonged to the Warcop family. Nicholson and Burn refer to Thomas Warcop of Lamberseat. It is the earliest known residence of the Whartons or de Quertons as it was originally written. It was from Lammerside Castle that this family moved to Wharton Hall. It is not as grand a pele tower as Pendragon Castle, nor is it so well sited. Pennant in his *Tour from Downing to Alston* (1801) says, "I proceeded from Wharton Hall along a very narrow vale watered by the Eden, and passed by a very ancient square tower called Lammerside Hall, formerly by the sad name of the Dolorous Tower. Something was told me of a Sir Tarquin and a Sir Caledos so that probably the place had been the subject of dire contention."

Primitive people were living in Wharton parish long before Lammerside Castle was built: long before the Roman occupation, in fact. Implements found in and around their settlements and tumuli identify them as Bronze Age people who lived about 1,800 years BC and may still have been there right up to the Roman occupation. They were pastoral folk who had developed a kind of garden agriculture, using cultivation terraces or strip lynchets. These long, narrow terraces can be found in almost every parish of the Upper Eden Valley and are seen at their best in Wharton Hall Deer Park.

At Bullgill the road is exchanged for a walled green track and open fell is close. But before reaching it the Settle-Carlisle railway line is crossed. The bridge is sited 1.5 miles south of Kirkby Stephen West station on one of the longest runs between two stations along the line. Garsdale, the next station south of Kirkby Stephen West is 9.75 miles away from it. There was a real chance in 1884 that a station would be built in Mallerstang but shortage of cash prevented this happening. The Midland Railway agreed to provide it if the residents of Mallerstang would build a road to it at a cost of £2,000. Land for the site was provided by Lord Hothfield but cash for the road was not forthcoming so the deal fell through.

South bound trains enter Mallerstang three miles south of Kirkby Stephen West through the 424 yards long Birkett Tunnel. It is sited right on the Great Pennine Fault and perhaps this accounts for the geological confusion exposed when it was being excavated. Shale, magnesium and mountain limestone, grit, slate, iron, coal and workable veins of lead were all discovered in, according to Mr John S.Crossley, Midland's engineer-in-charge, "The most curious combination I have every seen."

Many of the navvies who worked on the construction of the line came from Ireland and Wales. They lived in hutted camps erected at intervals along the line. One of these camps was on Aisgill Moor: another was on Birkett Common.

It was a tough life. There was little glamour in sinking shafts for the foundations of viaduct piers, building embankments, boring tunnels and digging cuttings. The work was hard, dirty and frequently carried out under appalling weather conditions. Money was the big attraction: 10/- a day, on average, while the job lasted.

Accommodation was poor. Men doing preliminary site work lived either in tents or sod huts roofed with planks. Their supplies were delivered on the backs of donkeys. As the main workforce moved forward so did the living quarters, usually wooden huts. These were divided into three sections: sleeping quarters for the family, sleeping quarters for the lodgers and a combined kitchen and dining area.

Some of the men's wives made brave attempts to brighten up their cabins with pictures cut out from magazines and illustrated newspapers. They saw to the cooking, kept the fires burning and looked after the lodgers. But for many the harsh living conditions were just too much. Unable to cope they became sluttish. Others became ill and a lot died in a smallpox epidemic brought about by overcrowding and lack of hygiene.

Excessive working for excessive high wages enabled the navvies to drink to excess; and there were many to exploit them in their excesses. Drink became a consolation; and any excuse was used for one, from pay days to funerals. To restrain them was useless for this only made them more violent.

During the building of the line the population of Mallerstang doubled. It was a development the dales folk did not exactly relish. There was not a great deal of love lost between those gentle-mannered hill folk and the wild boyos from Ireland and the fiery Celts. There were times when progress was nil, but as time passed the line was pushed forward and beyond the vale. And as it did so a semblance of the old tranquillity returned to Mallerstang.

Despite its lonely location, William Mounsey's Jew Stone fell victim to some navvies from the Ais Gill shanty town who, because they were unable to decipher the Latin and Greek texts or to understand the symbols, smashed it in a senseless act of vandalism.

Travelling north, once Ais Gill summit (1,169ft.) is passed the Settle-Carlisle drops steadily all the way to Ormside. But it does not drop as steeply as the road so anyone having a train ride on this scenic line is given far better views across the vale to Mallerstang Edge than are to be had from the road.

But the views on foot as you cross over Wharton Fell and, after a short, steep climb, reach the summit of Little Fell, are even finer. The way ahead is along a gradual, downhill slope before the final steep climb to The Nab and across the flat plateau to the summit of Wild Boar Fell itself.

It is from the Nab, perched on the very edge of the escarpment at its highest point, that the best views are obtained. The summit of Wild Boar Fell, only twenty-eight feet higher than the Nab, is well back from the escarpment so the views are much less dramatic. Both viewpoints offer panoramic prospects but the Nab has an added ingredient - excitation. From there, much of the Upper Eden Valley is in view with Kirkby Stephen prominent and Cross Fell forming a backcloth. To westward the higher reaches of the Lune can be seen and the Howgills share the western horizon with the more distant Lakeland fells. To eastwards, over Abbotside Common Great Shunner Fell and Lovely Seat catch the eye while to the south splendid Ingleborough and Whernside stand proud and tall, framed by Swarth

Fell and Widdale Fell. Directly below, narrow Mallerstang vale stretches, gouged so dramatically out of the surrounding fells. Closer still, just beneath your feet, the slight mound with a cairn on it is a tumulus.

There have been days when I have stood on the Nab enveloped in thick mist; but when you climb Wild Boar Fell expecting to be rewarded with spectacular scenery it is advisable to choose a fine day.

A triangulation column with a wind shelter wrapped around it marks Wild Boar summit. The mountain's only tarn, Sand Tarn, lies to the west of it. Greenrigg Moss, a little lower down the fellside, holds just as much water but it is spread out more. Hikers tend to avoid this undefined boggy ground.

There are many ways down to the cottages which stand beside the B6259 at the head of Mallerstang. They all cross Aisgill Moor, and are undefined and all are over very rough ground. The one I have used several times is that favoured by those jolly Mallerstang Horseshoe and Nine Standards Yompers. It is not a direct route because before the descent proper is made, Swarth Fell and Swarth Fell Pike are visited.

From the two cairns on Swarth Fell Pike the hidden valley of Grisedale, the valley of the wild swine, can be clearly seen below the western side of the fell. It is well worth a visit sometime, not only because it is a green oasis enclosed by dour fells but because gamekeeper Richard Atkinson, the remarkable man who remains a burning legend throughout the western dales lived there and gave it his heart.

The way down from the two cairns to Ais Gill cottages has no definition and is as rough as can be; but at least you will give the curlews something to laugh at as you scramble along.

From Ais Gill cottages the farm road to Hellgill Farm first crosses the Settle-Carlisle line then comes close to and eventually crosses the infant Eden. Near where farm road and river lie side by side Hell Gill Foss, the highest waterfall on the Eden puts on a spectacular display. Water pouring over its rim falls some sixty feet in one straight drop.

A little further up is Hell Gill gorge, some ninety feet deep in places and narrow enough at the top for anyone lish enough and stupid to jump. The farm close to the downstream end of Hellgill is Hellgill

Farm. It used to be an inn during the days when the road bridging Hellgill was the only one through the vale.

The walk continues, climbing steadily, along the top of Hangingstone Scar. At a point about a quarter of a mile along it's rim, the way is due east for three quarters of a mile to where, at the head of Red Gill the source of the Eden is reached.

12: Black Fell Moss to Kirkby Stephen via Mallerstang Edge and the Nine Standards

Length of section:	10 miles
Distance walked from Rockcliffe via the Roman Road:	84 miles
Distance walked from Rockcliffe via Wild Boar Fell:	91 miles
Map:	O.S. Landranger 91 and 98
Handy hostelries:	Black Bull, Croglin, King's Arms, Pennine, White Lion. Numerous cafés.

Route Directions (See map page 161)

From the source of the Eden on Black Fell Moss go N.W. along a clearly seen ridge, Gregory Band, following cairns, to join a track coming uphill from the left at a cairn, where go right, uphill, following cairns, to the summit of High Seat. Here there is a choice of routes. Either go straight ahead, northwards, to the one mile distant cairn on High Pike Hill, from where follow a faint track, dropping steeply to swampy ground before climbing more gently to the B6270, clearly seen ahead. Turn left along it to a parking area near its summit. Or leave High Seat in a westerly direction, descending steeply, to where becks, cross rough ground. Continue northwards across wet, undefined coarse grassland, keeping close to the escarpment's rim. A tall, slender cairn, which you pass close to the edge of the escarpment is a good marker. Continue to Fell's End where, at the north-facing disused quarry, descend steeply, then climb along a green track to the B6270 at the parking area.

The way ahead, undefined, is northwards across a limestone pavement and between peat hags, passing the head of Dukerdale on the left and climbing to Nine Standards Rigg, at the N.W. end of which are the Nine Standards. The least boggy way down from the Nine Standards is S.S.W., undefined, towards the head of Dukerdale, over rough ground. Where, close to the steep top of the gill, a stone wall crosses your line of walk turn right along it on a clear green track. Once through a gate just beyond a bothy on your left the green track becomes metalled. Continue along it, round the side of Hartley

Birkett on your right, passing a side road to Fell House on your right and a large quarry on your left to drop steeply into Hartley. At the bottom of the steep hill into Hartley go left, over a footbridge across Birkett Beck, then right and first left at a T junction. Take the tarmac road uphill to a gate which go through and continue downhill towards Kirkby Stephen, seen ahead. Continue through a snicket gate, close to the river on your left, to Frank's Bridge, a twin-arched stone bridge, which cross. Bear right, up some steps, where turn right at the top, then left up a steep alley which leads to Kirkby Stephen market-place and the end of the walk.

The Background Story
It wasn't a day for standing still. The sky was clear and blue with little cloud but the wind, the lazy wind, was fresh and bitterly cold. I was standing just below the head of Red Gill with spring water bubbling around my boots. Here the Eden was at its narrowest: so slender it could be spanned by the width of one of my feet. There were other springs set at irregular intervals lower down the slope but the one where I stood was the main one, the real source of the river. This was the very place William Mounsey had sought in 1850 with conditions so different from today. When Stuart Dean and I retraced Mounsey's footsteps, we found a huge snowdrift covering the whole of the top end of Red Gill. It prevented us from standing where I stood now. This time it was different. With only stray pockets of snow persisting in deep, north-facing hollows the exact source was no longer hidden. It was there: it was real. I could see it, feel its coldness about my feet and now had positive proof that Stuart and I had been spot on. It was a happy situation, one worthy of a drop of the hard stuff. But I had none with me. I made do with tea from my flask.

I looked towards the steep north bank of Red Gill above which William Mounsey had erected his Jew Stone and where it had lain, broken, for so many years. The exact spot is marked by the beginnings of a cairn made by the late head of Kirkby Stephen Primary School, Mr F.W.Parrot, OBE. How sad, I thought, that despite the remoteness of the site, the stone had fallen victim to Victorian vandals.

The air was alive with the mellifluous fluting of curlews. A pair of them, snatched by the stiff breeze, tore past in low, easy flight and were gone: but for long seconds after their plaintive cries lingered, giving sweet counterpoint to the infant Eden's babble.

While gathering strength on lonely, squelchy Black Fell Moss, the beck tumbles along its stony bed as Red Gill Beck; but even in its infancy it displays many of the impressive characteristics of the fair Eden it will become.

According to some authorities the name Eden is derived from the Anglo-Saxon words *ea* (water) and *dun* (a deep rooted valley). The oldest spelling of the river was Ptolemy's Greek version, the British form of which, according to Ekwall, is Ituna. This became Iduna, which in Old English was adopted as Idun that, with backmutation became Eodon. In Middle English this became Eden meaning water. Phillips in *Rivers and Mountains of Yorkshire* maintains that it is a corruption of the Celtic *ed-dain* meaning gliding stream.

William Camden, the sixteenth century antiquary and historian praises the river: "The most noble river in this county is the Eden, called by Ptolemy, Ituna. It rises at a place called Hugh-Seat-Morvill, or Hugh Morvill's hill, out of which two other rivers, Eure and Swale, run into Yorkshire. In its course, which is long, it receives no less than twelve rivers and brooks and some of them comfortable streams, so that it is a very large river before it comes to join the Eamont."

I share his view that the Eden is Westmorland's most noble river but cannot agree that Ure and Swale rise on Hugh Seat. Although the Ure and Hell Gill Beck, which Red Gill Beck becomes before being named Eden, flow parallel for a mile their respective sources are not close. The Ure is born in marshy ground on the western flank of the Ure Head 1.5 miles south of Huge Seat. The nearest tributary of the Swale to Hugh Seat is Great Sleddale Beck and several sikes drain into it from the eastern slopes of Black Fell Moss. Great Sleddale Beck and Birkdale Beck merge to become the Swale some 2.5 miles N.E. of Huge Seat.

If you stand at the source of the Eden, the peak directly in front of you to the south-east is Hugh Seat. In 1664 Lady Anne Clifford erected a boundary marker on it which became known as Lady Anne's Pillar. It is not at the summit, which is 2,257 feet above sea level. It stands a little lower down, around the 2,200 feet contour. For some years prior to 1953 it had been ruinous when, on August 3rd of that year Rev. John Breay and two helpers repaired it; and a jolly good job they made of it, too.

William Camden wasn't too keen on Black Fell Moss. It was, he recorded: "Such a dreary waste and horrid silent wilderness that certain rivulets that creep here are called Hell-becks, rivers of hell. In this part the goats, deer and stags of extraordinary size with branching horns find a secure retreat."

Four hundred years later many of Black Fell Moss's features are little changed: the peat hags remain, the distant landmarks stand as proud as ever and the fell is just as lonely. There is about it an ambience of timelessness. But change there is because today the fells are subject to intensive farming of one kind or another.

Neither goats nor deer and stags wander on Black Fell Moss these days; but sheep do. Usually they are Swaledales and they keep to their own heafs. The ratio is roughly one sheep to four or five acres.

Fellside farming is a rigorous and demanding life. From January to March much time is spent simply surviving winter hardships, looking after the sheep, feeding them and, when there has been a "hap-up," digging them out of snowdrifts and bringing the weak ones back to the farm to recuperate. On Black Fell Moss winter often extends into April. Sheep dipping takes place in April and by the middle of the month work continues round the clock as lambing time begins. In May the new lambs are castrated, vaccinated, dye-marked and their ears are nicked to establish ownership. During July and August the sheep are sheared and dipped and strays are gathered in. September and October are the months of the annual sheep sales. By the middle of November the tups are run with the ewes to produce next year's lambs. This is always later on the fells than on valley-bottom farms so that by the time the lambs are born it is hoped that the worst of the winter weather will have passed giving them a greater chance of survival. During February and March, when the fells offer least food, feed blocks are used to supplement the diet of the pregnant ewes.

While managing his fell sheep flock the farmer also has to carry out his arable farming. If he is sowing root crops for winter feed this is done during May. June sees the shearing of his valley-bottom sheep and, if the weather has been reasonable, early July is haytime. If he goes in for corn this increases his work load accordingly. Yes! It's a tough life being a fellside farmer, that's for sure.

I cannot imagine anyone reaching the source of the Eden not wanting to continue over Hugh Seat to visit Lady Anne's Pillar: the two are only about 500 yards apart.

Unlike any of the other cairns along Mallerstang Edge, Lady Anne's Pillar is made of squared stones. The one inscribed AP 1664 faces west and is easily recognised. AP stands for Anne Pembroke. The views from it are simply glorious. The Lakeland fells are over to westward while to the south the famous Three Peaks, Whernside, Ingleborough and Pen-y-Ghent, are clearly seen.

To the north of Black Fell Moss, running roughly N.W., there is a rocky outcrop called Gregory Band. The way across it is marked by cairns, which continue at irregular intervals along the full length of Mallerstang Edge. Those at the Nateby-Keld road end are shown on the map as "pile of stones" and those on Gregory Band as "currick." Since both descriptions are just alternative names for cairn it is something of a mystery that the terminology should change here. One of the cairns on Gregory Band is a tall, slender column around which a windbreak has been built. It makes a good butty stop.

The Yomp route is regained at Steddale Mouth from where the way is uphill to High Seat which at 2,328 feet is the highest point along the walk. From there you have a choice of routes, the higher and more direct one being along the top of the ridge, due north to one mile distant High Pike Hill, descending gradually. From the cairn on High Pike Hill a steep track leads to the B6270, an unfenced road across the moors between Nateby and Keld. The alternative is more devious, much more exciting and very much wetter. If your feet are still dry they probably won't be for much longer. If they are already squelchy, extra wetness will not make the slightest difference. Besides, a little pedal discomfort is a small price to pay for the superb views the slightly lower level edge walk has on offer.

From the cairns on High Seat the way is briefly westward, dropping steeply to some becks breaking up the ground in front of you prior to pouring over the rim of Mallerstang Edge, often to be blown back on themselves as spray by the very strong prevailing westerlies. The views are terrific and stay with you as you splash across the spongy fellside.

The Settle-Carlisle line is seen to advantage tunnels and all, as it skirts Wild Boar Fell. The road from Ravenstonedale is easily identified, as is Pendragon Castle on its mound beside the Eden.

A touch of character enhances a rather superior cairn that stands close to the crest of the escarpment just south of some long abandoned quarries. The "throughs" are built into it so that they become a staircase spiralling clockwise upwards. They can be climbed but doing so is hazardous for they are wildly spaced and the column narrows steadily between bottom and top. Then, having got there it is the devil's own job descending for fear of falling off.

As recently as the last century copper, tin and lead were worked in Mallerstang but only the lead mine was profitable. Coal was mined on the lower slopes of Mallerstang Edge, on the common above Outhgill. But the yield was poor and hardly sufficient for the needs of the inhabitants of the dale.

What induced men to quarry just below the rim of Mallerstang Edge is conjecture. Maybe the stone had special qualities. It can hardly have been a case of distance lending enchantment. One thing is certain, both about the quarries overlooking Mallerstang and the one high up on steep Fell's End, overlooking Tailbridge Hill; somebody had to climb a long way to get the stone.

Fell's End is very steep and the view from the top of it is breathtaking. To northwards lie the Pennines with Cross Fell, their highest point, prominent. To westward are High Street with Helvellyn and the peaks of central Lakeland. If you can see any smoke in the gap between the Pennines and the Lakeland fells, there lies Penrith.

The Nateby-Keld road crosses the Cumbria-Yorkshire boundary about half a mile east of Tailbrig - locals, like me, prefer the vernacular "Tailbrig" to the pedantic "Tailbridge Hill" - at a place called Hollow Mill Cross. No cross remains today, which is a pity for it would mark the site of the brutal murder in 1664 of a hosier, John Smith.

One enigma leads to another; and this one is known by the collective name the Nine Standards. From the Nateby to Keld road the way to it is northwards across a limestone pavement between peat hags, past the head of Rigg Beck and on to Nine Standards Rigg. There you will find three features: an O.S. Trig Point: a direction finder on a stone cairn and the Nine Standards. If you miss all three you are lost.

The direction finder was put there by Kirkby Stephen Fell Search Team to commemorate the wedding of Prince Charles and Lady Diana Spencer and was unveiled by W.R.Mitchell, then editor of the two admirable magazines that, between them, reflect northern life,

Cumbria and *The Dalesman.*

There is nothing mysterious about the view from the Nine Standards, unless they are curtained by mist and you can't see a thing. On a clear day all, or almost all, is revealed. The rounded Howgills are there, across the valley, as are many Lakeland peaks including Scafell Pike, High Street, Helvellyn, Blencathra and Carrock Fell. On a really clear day the Solway Firth shimmers in distant sunshine. But it is the Pennines themselves, spreading all around, and the beautiful Eden Valley, lying alongside them to westward, that hold the eye.

The mystery lies in the name itself. It is not known when the Nine Standards were built and some of the reasons given for their being where they are do not make much sense. The most popular legend is that they were built to give marauding Scots the impression that an English army was encamped there. But this is too fanciful to be taken seriously. The notion that there are nine standards because Roman soldiers always walked nine abreast just does not stand up to reality. There were Romans in the Eden Valley, to be sure, but the closest they got to the Nine Standards - which in any case had not been built at that time - was Brough *(Verterae)*. Nor does the word standard have any Roman association. It comes from the Early Modern English word *stander* meaning upright pillar and it was most likely adopted from its use as a mining term for a column of mineral left to support the ceiling of a mine. My view is that they are boundary stones that were enlarged by shepherds with time on their hands. Before the sheep were "heafed" shepherds spent a lot of time looking after the flocks and embellishing the standards helped to pass the time. These huge cairns were not simply thrown together: they were built.

Similar concentrations of cairns litter many heights both on the Pennines and through Lakeland. Some, like those on Cross Fell, mark neither summit nor boundary. They were built for no other reason than that shepherds had time on their hands and building material was available.

While a shadow of doubt remains so does the enigma. This adds flavour to the folklore of the area because everyone loves a mystery. And the Nine Standards straddle the skyline, an undated landmark.

But that is not the end of the story. Speculating on the name, Mr F.W.Parrot, OBE, Head of Kirkby Stephen Primary School for 38 years, saw in the NIne Standards a means of teaching Christian values. In many ways a man ahead of his time, he looked upon knowledge of the environment as being just as important as the three R's.

One Sunday, having done a great deal of writing, he was urged by his wife to go for a walk. He set off with no clear destination in mind and gravitated to the Nine Standards. In those days school classes were known as standards. Pupils began in Standard 1 and progressed through standard's 2, 3, etc. during their school life. There were other standards too: standard bread and standard cars. Making his way home from the Nine Standards he became deep in thought. Part of a passage of Scripture came to mind: "The fruit of the spirit is love, joy ....." The rest escaped him. Back home he looked it up and found that there were nine beatitudes, nine standards. He had found the basis of an address, which he gave many times in Methodist and Baptist chapels. He would urge people in Kirkby Stephen to remember, whenever they looked at the Nine Standards, which can be seen from many places in the town, that there are nine Christian standards. So, as a result of Mr Parrot's memorable Sunday walk the Nine Standards have become more than county boundary cairns. They now serve as a reminder that the whole Christian concept is held together by nine standards.

Rigg Beck, which rises at the head of Dukerdale near the Nine Standards, loses much of its water along wooden troughs at the S.W. corner of the Out wood, where holly trees grow in profusion in thin soil on a limestone bedrock. The channelled water gives Hartley its domestic water supply; what's left is allowed to run through pipes to become lost in Birkett Beck. This lively stream flows right down the middle of the village to Hartley Fold Farm at its northern limit; from where it curves west to join, after half a mile, the Eden at Low Mill.

Hartley is small and picturesque. It has a hill at its southern end on which once sat Hartley Castle, one of the homes of Andrew de Harcla. Between Birkett Beck, as it flows through the village, and the Eden there is a curving tongue of land beginning with the knoll on which the castle once stood and ending on level ground between Hartley Fold Farm and Low Mill. It is from this piece of land that both the de Harcla and the village names are derived. Hartley is obscure Old English derived from *harao* meaning wood and *cla* meaning something cloven which is well enough evidenced in place-names usage. It denotes "a tongue of land between two streams" or "a low curving hill projecting into flat ground." This fits the piece of land exactly.

What water is not diverted at the troughs continues along Rigg Beck, cascading down its steep limestone bed to flow along the foot of Ewebank Scaur. For a while its progress is gentle, from pool to pool. Then suddenly, at a bend in the cliff, the earth falls away and the beck pours down a steep rock face into a dub from where another small fall takes it clear of the cliff. Following heavy rain the foot of Ewebank Scaur can be dangerous. Downstream of the Scaur further progress is a gentle meander through beautiful woods, passing under a viaduct that once carried the railway over Stainmore. Then having left the limestone behind it meets the Eden on a sandstone bed at Turn Wheel which means "a loop in the river."

A most pleasant way from Hartley to Kirkby Stephen is over Gramskeugh, which is Old Norse from "demon-haunted wood." Perhaps in the far distant past the name fitted: the Norsemen were generally spot on with their place-names. I was born and bred in a house near the river and have always known it as Open Pasture. Times change - place-names stick.

The path leads invitingly down to the river, follows it briefly, then crosses it on a lovely two-arched stone footbridge. It winds between ancient buildings, up flagged steps and a wynd into the town.

Envoi

Shalom Hermon, a well-known tour guide in Israel, made an off-the-beaten track tour of England during September 1989. The tour emphasised sites connected with Jerusalem, Israel and the Jews and revealed common roots and links between England and Israel from the time of the Roman Empire to the present.

While he was a soldier in the Jewish Brigade during the Second World War, Shalom Hermon was stationed in England and spent his free time visiting various sites which have strong connections with the Holy Land. His major quest was to find the famous "Jew Stone" which had been on the bank of Eden River. It was only forty year later, during another visit, that he finally found the stone. On September 21st the stone was rededicated at Outhgill in Mallerstang.

An Informative sign, being prepared to stand alongside the Jew Stone, contains a section written in Hebrew with an English translation. It reads as follows.

Is The Stone Jewish?

In 1945 during World War II, *Shalom Hermon,* from the Jewish Brigade, did his artillery officer's training at Catterick Camp not far from here to the east. During the many exercises in Swaledale and on his many week-end hikes he came across the name "Jew Stone" on one of the maps. His curiosity to find the Stone was stilled only nearly forty years later when in 1984 he and his wife, Dvora, now living in Jerusalem, while looking for the Stone, found it at the farm of Mr and Mrs Thompson at Hanging Lund. Shalom decided that, despite William Mounsey not having been Jewish, the stone was Jewish. (What is "our dear native land?" "Why the Star of David?") and that the Stone was given the historical mission of being a link between the Jewish people and this beautiful part of England. Shalom donated an appreciable sum towards the restoration and re-erection of the Stone together with the Thompsons and Charlie Emett.

Is it mere chance that *Shalom* (in Hebrew peace) and *Emett* (in Hebrew truth) worked together to rebuild this wonderful monument at this beautiful site?

Selected Bibliography

Whellan, William	History and Topography of Cumberland and Westmorland	W.Whellan & Co.	1860
Robinson, William	A History of Man in the Lake District	Dent	1967
White, T.A.	The Once and Future King	Collins	1939
MacCana, Proinsias	Celtic Mythology	Hamlyn	1970
Kirby, D.P.	The Making of Early England	Batsford	1976
Graham, Frank	The Roman Wall: Comprehensive History and Guide	Frank Graham	1979
Smith, Kenneth	Carlisle	Dalesman Publ. Co. Ltd.	1970
Lyons, Nick (Ed.)	Fisherman's Bounty	W.H.Allen	1971
Evans, Eunice	Through the Years with Romany	University of London Press Ltd.	1946
Smith, A.H.	The Place Name of Westmorland Parts I and II	Cambridge University Press	1967
Sowerby, R.R.	Historical Kirkby Stephen and	Titus Wilson	

OTHER CICERONE BOOKS by CHARLIE EMETT

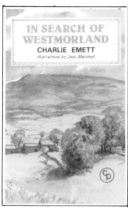

IN SEARCH OF WESTMORLAND

Illustrated by Jean Marshall

This book describes a circular walk more or less around the boundary of the old county of Westmorland.

Charlie Emett has a talent for bringing the historical background to life with a rich flow of anecdotes. Anyone who is fond of Westmorland will love this book.

Jean Marshall's pen sketches and watercolour cover add a delicate charm.

ISBN 0 902363 66 2   200pp
Card cover   £4.95

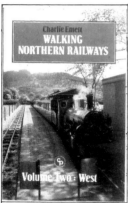

WALKING NORTHERN RAILWAYS
Volume 1: East

ISBN 0 902363 76 X 160pp
Card cover   £4.95

WALKING NORTHERN RAILWAYS
Volume 2: West

ISBN 1 85284 006 4 256pp
Card cover   £5.95

Volume 1 covers the east side of the Pennines from the Humber to the Scottish Border. Volume 2 covers west of the Pennines from Cheshire to the Border.

Charlie Emett's lifelong railway enthusiasm is reflected in these books, written in Charlie's entertaining style. All the old lines are documented, each with an historical introduction and background story; and a description of the present scene, with information on walking possibilities.
Several old lines are now walking or nature trails.

CICERONE PRESS
MILNTHORPE, CUMBRIA

PRINTED BY CARNMOR PRINT & DESIGN
95/97 LONDON ROAD, PRESTON, LANCASHIRE, ENGLAND